S0-BEZ-042

BARRON'S
A BUSINESS
SUCCESS GUIDE

Creative Problem Solving

By

Donald J. Noone, Ph.D.

BARRON'S

DEDICATION

To my two sons, Don and Seth, from whom I have learned so much.

© Copyright 1993 by Barron's Educational Series, Inc.

All inquiries should be addressed to:
Barron's Educational Series, Inc.
250 Wireless Boulevard
Hauppauge, New York 11788

Library of Congress Catalog Card No. 92-34642

International Standard Book No. 0-8120-1461-8

Library of Congress Cataloging-in-Publication Data

Noone, Donald J.
    Creative problem solving : a business success guide / by Donald J. Noone.
        p.   cm.
    "Barron's educational series."
    Includes index.
    ISBN 0-8120-1461-8
    1. Problem solving.   2. Creative ability in business.   I. Title.
HD30.29.N66   1993
658.4'09—dc20   92-34642
                                                        CIP

PRINTED IN THE UNITED STATES OF AMERICA

56   5500   987654

CONTENTS

INTRODUCTION

To succeed in business and life many skills are necessary, but the skill that cuts across every challenge is the ability to solve problems. If you are inept or mediocre in solving problems you will not succeed in business. Why? Because problems are everywhere; nothing is nailed down, and new challenges, concerns, irritations, or opportunities confront us every single day. Whether the problem is competition, customer satisfaction, obsolescence, unemployment, motivation, time use, money, people, relationships, or your own health and well being, all of these problems occur and recur periodically.

Since no one is going to come down the pike and tell you what you should do about these problems, you need to figure it out yourself. Unfortunately, there is no fairy godmother to sprinkle fu-fu dust on your head to make the pain go away. To paraphrase Harry Truman—the buck stops with yourself.

How to solve problems better, more creatively, more effectively, thus becomes a high priority for all businesspeople. How you do this is what this little book is all about. It contains a body of knowledge that, if mastered, can enhance your creativity and give you powerful tools you can use the rest of your life in every area of your life. It can help lead you to success not only in business, but in the quality of your life on this planet.

The approach here is a holistic one. It does not deal with just problem-solving techniques, but with the whole person—your beliefs, your attitudes, your body, and your energy. How to encourage you, the problem solver, to fine-tune your capability is as important as technique. As a consequence, you will see the payoffs for this approach go far beyond problem solving. When you apply the strategies suggested, the proof will become self-evident.

CHAPTER 1

THE PROBLEM SOLVER AS THE PROBLEM

Personal Impediments to Solving Problems

"Man is his own worst enemy."

—Cicero

Why do we have problems? Mainly because we live in an imperfect, unfinished universe. Everything is in constant flux; nothing is nailed down "once and for all."

Change is the order of the day. Our planet is populated by imperfect people with imperfect plans that are imperfectly executed. On top of this are legions of "true believers" with tunnel vision who know there is only one answer—and that they have it!

This is complicated by the observation that talent, intelligence, caring, creativity, and inventiveness are not equally distributed; nor are the resources of the world—food, raw materials, rain, and other natural assets. All this leads to scarcity, coupled with man's pursuit of abundance. In many cases, the men who undertake this pursuit are less than angels—venal, self-seeking, lying, cheating, rapacious types who exploit, intimidate, and persecute others. In the meantime, babies are born, get sick, recover, mature, learn how to survive, grow old, and eventually die. This gets aggravated by the accidents and chance in life, multiplied by civil unrest, acts of God, and natural catastrophes.

Problems? Isn't it a wonder we have so few problems. Problems are part of the human condition.

Descartes said: "*Cogito, ergo sum*"—"I think, therefore I am." A more accurate proof of existence would be: "I have problems, therefore I am." The day that you or we, have no problems is the day we no longer breathe. Problems come with the territory. *The ability to solve problems is your key to success, to real power; and to happiness and fulfillment as a human being.*

But problem solving ability can be impaired, and many of us are not very good at solving our own problems, much less those of the world. A lot of times we get in our own way. So, before I give you a model that can help you become a creative problem solver, let's take a look at the dark side—at four reasons why a person's problem-solving ability might be impaired. By examining these four factors, you will see people you know, and paths to avoid.

The four key impediments demonstrated by impaired problem solvers are:

Inhibiting Beliefs
Go Nowhere Questions
An Impaired Instrument
Ignorance Of Problem-Solving Techniques

SOME KEY INHIBITING BELIEFS AND CONSEQUENCES

There are many inhibiting beliefs that prevent creative problem solving. I have grouped many of the key ones into eight types of impaired problem solvers: The Dictator; The Blamer; The Absurdist; The Victim; The Perfectionist; The Jelly Fish; The Chameleon and The Resister. Identifying them and their beliefs is to expose paths we do not want to follow.

1. *The Dictator*. The core belief of this type is "I know better." This kind of person is arrogant about solutions. Typically, these people believe they are surrounded by idiots, lesser mortals, or folks not endowed with their wisdom. Often they do not want to be confused with

facts, and impose their solutions on others, regardless of whether others like it or not. They regularly enforce their solutions by naked power, verbal abuse, or even physical violence. Anyone with a dissenting viewpoint is shot, e.g., whistleblowers and messengers bearing bad tidings need to be well-insured. In organizations where this authoritarian type exists, the members feel intimidated, paranoic, and blocked. There is typically a party line, and deviation is secretive. PYA (Protect Your Assets) is the modus operandi, with "signoffs" at every level needed before a decision is made.

The Dictator exemplifies tunnel vision. People of this type typically hop on the first solution that comes to mind, and close the door on any alternatives. Creativity goes south, and sloshing through the swamp is the effect. Ridicule greets any disagreement or suggestion for improvement. In straight-jacket organizations where this is typical, the creative types invariably head for the exit, while the eyes of other employees begin to glaze over. "Yes men" advance in their careers, and the organization starts the greasy slide toward mediocrity.

2. *The Blamer.* These people believe that nothing is ever their fault. They typically abdicate responsibility for a problem (and, of course, for the solution). Their reflex response, when a problem occurs, is to go on a witch hunt and to point an accusing finger at someone else. Psychic energy gets so wrapped up in the attack that they have precious little left for creative problem solving. It's as if their problem is solved once they nail it on someone else's door.

The difficulty with this strategy as a problem-solving technique is that the original problem usually gets worse. When this behavior occurs in organizations, employees usually go into hiding; and the pressure to lie, massage the facts, and to take no risks is profound.

3. *The Absurdist.* People of this type embrace the irrational. Why? Because, when something has happened, their immediate response is to say, "It shouldn't have

happened!" It is not possible for something that has happened to "shouldn't have." These words are usually a cover for heavy emotion, such as frustration, anger, or disappointment. In effect, these people just stamp their feet on the ground like a horse and go nowhere. The words "it shouldn't have happened" are really a condemning judgment of the situation. Condemning judgments invariably unleash a flood of emotion and mire a person in pain. Some people have spent lifetimes in dealing with problems this way. What do they get for all their anguish? Nothing but more anguish.

4. *The Victim.* "It's not fair. Why me? Other people live blissful, trouble-free lives. Why can't I? I don't deserve these problems." All problems, large or small, are onerous to this person. They don't know why they have to be inconvenienced by their troubles. When they do have problems, they are quick to cry to the heavens over their lot. They go through life feeling victimized, and even get angry at the gods for sticking it to them. The beauty of their viewpoint is that, once they utter their judgment of inequity, they are off the hook—they do not have to do anything about their situation. Their solution is their moral indignation.

5. *The Perfectionist.* "The solution must be perfect." This is a core belief of perfectionists. The problem with this belief is that it is irrational. Why? When it comes to human behavior, there is no perfection. It is simply not possible to do anything perfectly. Everything can be improved. There is no one right way to do anything. As a consequence, the solutions these people come up with to solve their problems are never good enough. All they focus on is the deficit, the lack, the shortfall. As a result, they are invariably miserable creatures. Sometimes they simply impose this trip on themselves; most of the time they inflict it on everyone around. Since they are surrounded by inept mortals, who regularly do not deliver perfection, these pitiful creatures become the target for opprobrium on a routine basis.

Actually, two things happen: the perfectionists inflict condemning judgments on themselves, and they reverse the "golden rule"—they do unto others as they do unto themselves. With all their energies tied up in criticism, they invariably don't have much left over to solve problems. Since everything has failure written all over it, even before they start, they often don't. Rather, procrastination, fire fighting, loneliness and crisis management, become their lot in life.

6. *The Jelly Fish*. These people are committed to waiting. They have learned that it is less painful to stay in neutral than to accelerate and run a risk of getting a ticket. The fast lane scares them. And if they do get in gear, the minimum speed is just fine for them. Take no risks and you face no risks. Observe every traffic sign. In their education they have likely acquired one virtue—obedience.

This type is a great operative in a bureaucracy where procedure and policy are spelled out and all they have to do is follow the rules. However, give them an unexpected challenge and like a turtle under siege, they simply retract their heads into their shells. This is the type that would have been rearranging the deck chairs on the Titanic, shining brass while the ship was sinking; or would have been making buggy whips long after Ford replaced the wagon. They purposefully ignore one of life's basic principles, "no risk, no growth."

Instead, they invariably set themselves up for a greater failure. In effect, they are like the bike rider who stops pedaling—they fall over. Their fear and passivity become their impetus for embracing ideologies, leaders, and groups that claim they do know. As a consequence, they are prime candidates for becoming "true believers" and are often exploited, led into dark alleys and mugged.

7. *The Chameleon*. These are the professional people pleasers in life. They have such a pitifully low sense of self-esteem that they grovel to have someone smile at

them, approve of them, or accept them. So, when confronted with a problem, instead of looking inside for possible solutions, they take their cues from others. They never come up with their own solutions to problems. They make a habit of wetting their fingers, and holding them up in the air to gauge which way the wind is blowing. They are the typical "yes men," and "right on!" is their usual chorus. For them, interpersonal affirmation by others is their primary value while personal inventiveness remains locked up. They are the part of the crowd that will agree that the emperor does have clothes on.

In organizations these people are temporizers and quick-change artists and blend into the surroundings. It is no wonder that in business service is so bad, products break and companies fold. Honesty, the real truth, and having the courage of their convictions is OK for heroes; survival is the name of this person's game.

8. *The Resister.* People of this type hate change, love comfort, routine, and the predictable. They are committed to the status quo. They have a deep attachment to order, organization, and the familiar. Anything that disrupts their "steady state" world is anathema. It deserves to be attacked, avoided, ignored, eliminated, or diluted. Comfort is the criterion for a good idea, not improvement, progress, better service, or the greater good of the organization.

In bureaucracies this is probably the most common syndrome of employees. How do we know? Introducing something new, such as computers, typically encounters massive resistance and, although employees know that computers will eliminate the drudgery of their paperwork, large numbers of them prefer familiar misery to the ease that comes through learning something new. This kind of person defines change as the enemy. When problems arise, they curse the problem, curse the situation, and invariably apply tired rules that don't quite fit. The result is that they are frequently angry, and those who use their service develop scars dealing with them.

There are many other types of impaired problem solvers and beliefs that support ineptitude in problem solving. Whatever they are, they all tend to shut down creativity, not only in the problem solver, but for others in an organization. How not to go down these paths is the subject of the next chapter.

GO NOWHERE QUESTIONS

The kind of questions a person asks dictates the quality of that person's life, his problem-solving capability, and the degree of creativity of solutions. The person with an impaired problem-solving capability asks questions that do not stimulate creativity, but rather ones that "go nowhere," or to the wrong place.

1. *Endless Loop Questions.* This is the kind of question that does not put a person on a growth trajectory but cements him into powerlessness. For example, when a problem occurs, this person exclaims: "Why me?" "Why did it have to happen?" "Why, why, why?" Often his eyes are rolled back in his head as he addresses this to the heavens.

The problem is that this is not a real question searching for real information, but rather an emotional cry of pain that expresses how badly he feels, how angry he is, or how unfairly he has been treated. It is the cry of a victim—confused, powerless, and hurt. Some people spend a lifetime lamenting the loss of a loved one, or some other catastrophic experience, and all they get each time they utter this "endless loop question" is more pain, anguish, and frustration. The more the "endless loop" question is asked, the more it reinforces itself.

2. *The Wrong Questions.* These are questions that miss the point of the problem and offer no sense of what a good solution would look like. These folks would ask, "Where is the fiddle?" while Rome burned. They wonder "which mattress should I put my money under?" while inflation eats away its value. They investigate

"which cigarette tastes better?" while their life span is shortened by six years. Or perhaps they would focus on "how much to lower prices and build market share?" while cash and profitability evaporate. These people do not know how to think about a problem, or a solution, and, as a result, invariably create bigger problems for themselves. How to ask "right" questions is fundamentally what this book is all about.

AN IMPAIRED INSTRUMENT

There is another dimension to problem solving typically overlooked because it operates at an unconscious level. But it has everything to do with the creativity of the problem solver, and that is an appreciation of the body. Just as a well-made, properly tuned violin dictates whether or not beautiful music can be produced, your body is the instrument that will condition the quality of creative output in problem solving.

By your body, we mean the problem solver's posture, gestures, feelings and energy level. The physiological cues your body emits are mainline messages to the brain. For example, if you sit in a chair with your shoulders slumped, and a frown on your face, and hold that posture for a couple of minutes, your brain will associate those cues with sadness. You will then get flooded with sad feelings, and your problem-solving capability will diminish straightaway. Why? Because there is an inverse correlation between heavy negative feelings, and having the problem-solving capability of your brain available. Likewise, your energy is what supports your health and your drive. When energy is down, problem-solving capability is low. People with impaired problem-solving capabilities are invariably ignorant of how to sustain high levels of energy, or deny that it has anything to do with personal effectiveness. They don't know how to breathe, eat properly, or exercise sufficiently to maximize energy. They are eight-cylinder machines with only four cylinders working.

IGNORANCE OF PROBLEM-SOLVING TECHNIQUES

Up to now we've focused on deficiencies in the problem solver. But even if you have the right beliefs, do not resort to endless loop questions, do not ask the wrong questions, or are in tip-top physical condition, you still need to master the techniques of problem solving. Without an understanding of the conditions of creativity, brainstorming, questioning, mind maps, association, analogy, fantasy, relaxation, role play, or Quantum Leap Thinking, a problem solver will wind up mining dirt and never reach the gold.

Unfortunately, these techniques are not widely taught in schools, and only haphazardly in business. In fact, there is a mighty prejudice against anything new, different, unfamiliar, unique or creative. So, even equipped with the tools and techniques, the problem solver will need to battle resistance. Part of the goal here will be to help you do so. However, don't let this preview of coming attractions daunt you. Problem solving is fun; creativity is a form of play. So look forward to a playful romp through this book. You will learn how to dance through the resistance, and come up with ingenious solutions to your problems.

When you understand and practice the problem-solving model I developed here, you will experience real power. Why? Real power is not money, position, or degrees. *Real power is possessing the creative ingenuity to solve problems.* With it, your self esteem will improve; your confidence will climb; and your willingness to take risks and lead will be strengthened. The key to your future is your ability to solve problems, and from that all good things will flow.

I am delighted I can share this knowledge with you!

CHAPTER 2

BELIEFS THAT LIBERATE

The Right Attitude is the Lever

BARRON'S BUSINESS SUCCESS SERIES

*"The creative mind is like a
parachute; it has to be opened to be of
any use."*

—Anonymous

Beliefs are important because they allow a person to know what meaning an experience has. Just as beauty is in the eyes of the beholder, so is ugliness, and so is moral goodness, or badness. The human experience is interpreted through a person's belief system and, although most things lie outside of a person's brain, everything is filtered through beliefs. It is beliefs that give a phenomenon meaning. So when it comes to change, problems, obstacles, pain, or the like, what we think, what we believe about them, can be either an energizing experience or a depressing one.

In Chapter 1 some of the beliefs that inhibit problem-solving capability were discussed. Now let's take a look at some beliefs that can support the creative problem solvers and put them into a more resourceful state.

STARE REALITY IN THE EYE

As a prelude to having supportive problem-solving beliefs, it is wise to stare stark reality in the eye and accept it. And what is that reality? The reality is that problems are a fact of life. The day you and I have no problems is the day we no longer breathe. Why? As we mentioned earlier, the reason is that everything in the universe is in constant flux, and nothing is ever nailed once and for all. When we think we have something really nailed, we really only have it nailed for today—maybe! Every solution to a problem is, therefore, tentative and subject to revision and improvement. What was true yesterday may not be tomorrow; what solved the problem yesterday may create a new problem and what gave us closure yesterday may become unhinged today. So, when one problem appears solved, another pops up. We never control everything; we never put everything in its place; we never rest thinking our work is done. That is reality.

This reality is not meant to depress you, but to get you to welcome change, to become energized by problems, and to drop into a problem-solving mode quickly when confronted with a problem.

PAYOFFS FOR SOLVING PROBLEMS

Why is this important? One of the great joys in life is solving problems. It is fun, it is stimulating, it is fulfilling (or, to be realistic, after you finish this book, it will be). It makes us feel truly human and truly alive. It gives us a sense of accomplishment and closure on an issue, albeit temporarily. The payoffs for solving problems allow progress and keep us at the cutting edge. Even when the problem is not fun, e.g., sickness problems, when solutions are found, relief from pain occurs and that is always welcomed.

THE BETTER PART OF WISDOM

What, therefore, is the better part of wisdom? Welcome problems and get into a problem-solving mode as soon as possible. Get on with it!

What is implicit in the previous statement is a core belief that will emancipate creativity. The core belief that propels the believer into creativity can be expressed a hundred ways—we will offer a few variations for your consideration:

I love problems.
Problems spell opportunity.
Problems are the prelude to progress.
Problems allow the expression of my power.
Problems tell me what I have to do.
Problems precede improvement.
Problems are fun.

What these imply is an acknowledgment of the reality of change. Change creates problems because what satisfied yesterday does not work today. So change is the reality, problems are the reality, and how you define something is your subjective reality. We can define change either as something positive and life enhancing, or as something awful. I maintain that it makes the most sense to define reality as good, change as good, problems as good, and that positive orientation will make the problem-solving process exhilarating. When you fall in love with change and greet problems as new friends, it becomes a self-empowering experience. So what is my advice?

Fall in love with problems.

An example of the consequences of this belief occurred to me recently. A client of mine had invited a group of high-powered customers to an event where they were asked to do two things: identify problems they had with his company's products and service, and recommend what he could do about them. Part of the intended result of the meeting was to strengthen relationships with the company and that was, indeed, accomplished.

However, when I chatted with the CEO after the event, he looked as if he had been hit by a truck and I asked him if something was troubling him. He said he was overwhelmed, felt alone, and that no one else cared about the business the way he did. He said the dream of building a great company was now becoming more like a pipe dream.

After I listened to him for a while, I encouraged him to reframe the experience he had just had and, in a while, he began to see the following: He now had a great opportunity to respond to these customers. He now knew what their problems were—unfiltered by others. He had really strengthened the company's relationships with these customers.

He opened the door wide for his own people and himself to recontact these customers on a more regular basis. He achieved great good will with the customers and they admired the courage he showed in fielding their recommendations on-the-spot. Some even thought they ought to have these sessions with their own customers.

He also realized he did, indeed, have a chance to explain the progress and direction of his company.

By changing his beliefs the sense of hopelessness evaporated, his spirits lifted, and he began to consider how he could exploit this opportunity in a meaningful way. Thus, he slipped into a problem-solving mode and began to think that "bad news gotten this way" was terrific and that he would go out and get the bad news all over the country.

This story really happened and shows the power of belief; how what you believe to be the case uplifts or grounds a person's energy and spirit.

THE SECOND GREAT LIBERATOR

The second great liberator of creativity is to suspend negative judgment when confronted with a problem or possible solutions.

First, what happens when judgment is not suspended?

A negative critical judgment closes the door on possibilities. It forecloses the creative process before it has a chance to evolve.

When directed at the problem (e.g., saying "It shouldn't have happened") such a judgment generates frustration and anger that impede progress in solving the problem. When directed at the cause of a problem, it is typically packaged in a condemning judgment that criticizes, blames, and distances the parties involved in the problem. When directed at the solution, it shuts down generation of better solutions and sets the critic up to embrace inadequate solutions, or shoots down ideas that might have merit.

So, like the parachute, keep the mind open by not passing judgment precipitously.

Related to this thought is a colloquial admonition: "Don't be a but-head." Although this phrase sounds like the slang young folks use when admonishing a pal for being stupid, what is meant here is to emphasize the killing effect the word "but" has as a response to any new idea or proposal, e.g., "I like the idea, *but* it won't work." "It's wonderful, *but* we tried it before." "It has merit, *but* it costs too much." "It's colorful, *but* it might be offensive."

In my experience "but" is like a stop sign, meaning, "Don't go any further and abandon the idea or the dream." "But" is often the slayer of dreams, the damper on the fire, and the favorite word of the negatives on the planet.

So, along with eschewing negativity and suspending critical judgment, beware of "but."

As a liberating tip, when you are tempted to use "but" in response to something new or different, use "and" instead, and notice the difference.

HAVE AN OPEN MIND

The flip side of being a negative, critical "but-head" is the open mind. An open mind is a mind that has learned how to suspend judgment and explore the problem and its dimensions. It is a mind that asks questions, whereas a closed mind has no questions, just the answer. The answer is a belief in the presumed superiority of a particular position.

Beware, the person who has *the* answer. People who have *the* answer no longer have questions. In fact, they are often intolerant of anyone who has questions.

Extremes in this absolutist embrace of truth were achieved during The Spanish Inquisition and, of late, by the Iranian death sentence for Salman Rushdie, who dared to question the manner in which Islamic Faith is practiced in his book, *Satanic Verses*.

People who have *the* answer to anything have closed the book and their mind on any other possibility. This can happen in any arena, religious, philosophical, aesthetic, political, educational, legal, as well as in such areas as fashion, style, and etiquette. It is equally true, of course, in business.

THE ANTIDOTE

What is an antidote to this tunnel vision? One such expanding belief is that "there is always another way." By implication it allows persons to be less positive about the belief that there is only one way—theirs! It may appear strange that advocating uncertainty can be a positive step, but it is. Why? It prods the mind to an improvement orientation. It forces the mind to be on the look out for another, and possibly better, way. It stimulates growth, expansiveness, ingenuity, and invention. It keeps a person open to other's thoughts and suggestions, and does not condemn ideas out of hand when they are different.

In a word, it promotes tolerance as well as receptivity to other approaches. When you hear yourself or someone else saying there is only one way to do this, you know that you, or they, are dead wrong. There is always another way, and that is the one you have not thought of yet.

TO ACHIEVE QUALITY GO FOR QUANTITY

Implicit in the previous discussion is another important axiom, one that has to do with the ability to choose. But first, imagine you want an apple and that you go into a supermarket to get one. You walk up to the fruit bin and you see there is only one apple there. How would you feel?

On the other hand, suppose you walk up to a fruit bin and the apples are piled in a high pyramid. What do you do? You scan the entire pile, pick up an apple, then another one and you compare your choices to many others. You might pick up a few more apples and examine them, but you will surely take with you the best apple.

Too often people try to solve problems with the first idea that comes to mind—invariably it is not the best.

The rule of thumb, therefore, in becoming a truly creative problem solver is to have a lot of ideas from which to choose. The chances of coming up with a quality solution are multiplied proportionately.

DIFFERENT IS NOT WRONG

Directly connected with this view, is another belief that supports the open mind: "Different is not wrong, just different." I should say in passing that occasionally different is wrong, in the case of unethical, illegal or criminal acts that are gross violations of human standards. However, apart from the relatively few instances that are readily apparent, overwhelmingly in the arena of other behaviors, choices, styles, attitudes, and the like, *different is just different*, and not wrong.

By maintaining this stance, the open mind is kept open and does not foreclose on other expressions of the human spirit. This allows a person to learn and explore other ways of thinking and behaving.

The saying at the beginning of the chapter, "The creative mind is like a parachute; it has to be opened to be of any use," is, again, very much to the point.

CREATIVITY AS PLAY

All of the comments above about openness, tolerance, entertaining differences, suspending negative critical judgment, and defining reality as good, change as good, and problems as good, are all the attributes associated with play.

Draw a picture in your mind of yourself playing a game such as basketball or golf when you were at your peak. Remember those times? You could hardly miss. You were in a flow; it was effortless; you were in the groove.

When this happens to athletes, they are invariably relaxed, focused, and the negative judgmental voice in their head is silent. These are the times when athletes are at their best.

That is the way creativity can be. That is the way problem solving can be. And as you define it, so it is, and will be.

Therefore, define problems and problem solving as: an adventure, an opportunity, a chance to grow, to stretch, to advance, to progress, to improve, to invent, to create, to be fulfilled, and particularly above all, as fun!

Your creative prowess will be released. You will be energized, and the solutions you generate will even surprise yourself.

You will have greater solutions now at your fingertips. You will indeed be playing at the top of your game, truly focused, truly relaxed, truly clear, truly in a dimension that will enhance your own endeavors and one that will stimulate and inspire you to even greater heights.

You will be pushing aside the negative aspects within yourself and simply targeting what has to be done. You will zero in on problems you previously thought were impossible to answer.

Try it. It does work. You will see solutions you never realized before.

That is the way creativity can be. That is the way problem-solving can be. It taps into the best part of you in a way that you hadn't seen previously.

And, there's nothing better than that.

CHAPTER 3

PROBLEM SOLVING—THE GREATEST SKILL OF ALL

Defining Our Terms

*"Sweet are the uses of adversity;
Which, like the toad, ugly and
venomous,
Wears yet a precious jewel in his head."*

—Shakespeare

It is useful to define our terms. Once they are clear,
the significance of what we are embarked upon will
stand in relief. Then the diamond will rotate and a
number of the facets can be explored for greater understanding. Greater understanding will lead to greater motivation to be a master problem solver.

WHAT IS A PROBLEM?

A problem is a situation that a person judges as bad, or
less ominously, as something that needs to be corrected.
A problem can be experienced in a variety of ways but
is looked on as a shortfall, a deficit, a lack, a dishar-
mony, a puzzlement, an inconvenience, a discomfort, or
a pain of some sort. A problem implies that a state of
wholeness does not exist, and "should" exist. A problem implies that it is desirable to achieve harmony, comfort, knowledge, certainty, or the goal or result intended.

WHO DECIDES THERE IS A PROBLEM?

Whenever a person observes a discrepancy between the
way things are and the way things ought to be, and

utters internally or in speech "that's bad, and it shouldn't be," the situation is perceived to be a problem and needs to be corrected. On the other hand, it is possible for a person to observe a discrepancy between "should" and reality and for it not to be a problem for that person. For example, suppose everyone is supposed to report to work at 9 AM and everyone does except John Smith, who comes in at 9:15 AM everyday. When a co-worker asks a secretary who is always on time, "Do you find his lateness is a problem?" she says, "No, it's not my problem."

So a discrepancy can exist "out there," but if a person does not define it as a problem, then it is not a problem for that person. What this means is that the secretary did not pass a condemning judgment on the situation. So, for her, his lateness just "is."

This idea implies that problems are in the eye of the beholder, so what is a problem for one person or group may not be a problem for another person or group. Whole cultures, in fact, like the Hindu culture can accept the status quo and never feel that something ought to be done about poverty, disease, filth, or the lot of women. Acceptance of what is can make for a problem-free existence but, when institutionalized, it becomes the basis for totalitarianism, slavery, and intellectual bondage. As a consequence, improvement in life or living conditions is foreign and the same pain thrives generation after generation. What supports the status quo is not allowing members of those societies to make any judgments of dissatisfaction. Such utterances of unhappiness would be considered subversive and would be severely punished. So people do not make them and the pain goes on.

On the other hand, when there is a discrepancy between a "need" or a "should" and a person says in effect "it ought not to be," the situation becomes a problem in search of a solution.

PROBLEM OWNERSHIP

Related to the idea that problems are in the eyes of the beholder, is an important question a problem solver needs to ask: "Who owns this problem?" The answer to this question is: I, you, we, or they. If I own the problem, I own the responsibility to find the solution. If you own the problem, it is your responsibility to find the solution. If we own the problem, we need to find a solution together. If they own the problem, they own the responsibility to find the solution.

Often good-hearted people want to own other people's problems—smother mothers/fathers, or over-controlling bosses, for example. The consequence of this approach is that a parent or a boss of this type is always stressed, as he takes the responsibility for solving everyone else's problems. This type winds up dictating; their children or direct reports wind up obeying and, in that act, become infantilized, never learning how to figure anything out on their own. Thus problem-solving abilities never get developed, creativity evaporates, and the birth and prevalence of stifling bureaucracy is explained.

WHERE DO PROBLEMS ARISE?

Problems can arise anywhere deficits occur: in racial, educational, political, medical, financial, recreational, religious, and familial arenas, for example. They can occur for individuals, groups, organizations, and societies. They can occur as a consequence of acts of God, such as earthquakes, floods, volcanic eruptions, snow, rain, sleet, heat or cold; or flow out of wars, civil unrest, ethnic strife, or political vendetta. Problems can arise out of scarcity and need. Problems can come from the deviance of others who cause havoc in other people's lives, such as murderers, thieves, muggers, liars, embezzlers, and criminals of all stripes. Problems can occur at any stage in a person's life cycle, from birth, to childhood, adolescence, maturity, middle age, or old age. And, of course, death is always a problem for individuals, groups, and societies.

The most emotionally challenging part of problems for an individual is that, more often than not, problems come as a surprise. Despite the ubiquity of problems, the unexpected or surprise element is what sets a person back, where precious time is lost and where the problem situation tends to get worse before it gets better.

By understanding the ubiquity of problems, and the predictability of problems, a person can go through life not cursing the darkness, but dealing with problems with the coolness and humanity of a professional problem solver. That is the intended result of this book.

THE CONNECTION BETWEEN PROBLEM AND SOLUTION

Understanding what constitutes a problem is important. Defining a situation as a problem is exciting because that very act of definition posits a need for a solution. To show you the intimate connection between the two, simply write down immediately what comes to mind after each of the five words that follow. Answer them as fast as possible; put down the first thing that pops into your mind:

Boy   _____
Shoe   _____
One   _____
Black   _____
Problem _____

Most of you after "problem" wrote down "solution" or "solve." This suggests we have deeply imbedded in our consciousness a drive for finding solutions when confronted with a problem. So, the first step in moving towards a solution is to start by defining the problem.

HOW DO YOU DEFINE A PROBLEM?

There are many ways to define a problem. The one that I find is the quickest path to creative thinking is to "start at the end." What is the end? That is the specific measurable result you want to achieve. When a person observes a deficit in some situation there is an intuitive image of a situation in the future where the deficit is removed and harmony or the goal is achieved.

To really make the search for a solution productive, it is helpful to know where you are going, to have a destination in mind, so that if it happened, you would be able to tell. For example, suppose you learn 53% of minorities up to age 45 are involved in the criminal justice system, either convicted, arrested, indicted, serving time, or paroled. You define this as a serious problem for society. A way to get on with the search for a solution is to start at the end. The end, the desirable result, would be to have a rate of participation in the criminal justice system no greater than that of majority males, which is 14%. So the goal or objective would be: Achieve 14% participation rate of minority males in the criminal justice system. The next step after stating the problem is to formulate the objective into a question, i.e., "How can we achieve a rate of participation of only 14% for minority males in the criminal justice system?"

Suppose 95% of the food sent for starving families in Ethiopia is stolen and sold on the black market for exorbitant profit. To make this a clear problem, ask: "How can we ensure that 100% of the food sent to starving families in Ethiopia is, indeed, delivered to them?"

Or suppose a company discovers sales volume is up but profitability is down. The desired goal would be to have sales volume and profitability up. So the problem might be: "How can we maintain high volume and, at the same time, high profit?"

WHY IS STARTING AT THE END SO VALUABLE?

We are cybernetic creatures. This means we are goal-oriented creatures. What motivates anyone is the pursuit of a goal. If you have ever come across someone suffering from ennui, lassitude, dissipation, or lethargy, I will show you a person with no meaningful goals. On the other hand, when persons have goals that they want to achieve, it ignites, it fires enthusiasm, it gets the creative wheels turning, it sets a challenge that stimulates. So a way to get right into a problem-solving mode with enthusiasm is to, paradoxically, start at the end; to have a reasonably clear image in mind of what a solution would look like if found.

Once the end is clear, then the creative challenge is to discover ways to make it happen.

So a solution to a problem would lead to the elimination of a deficit, or the achievement of a goal or state of harmony that had been in disequilibrium.

WHAT ARE SOLUTIONS?

Solutions are possibilities. Solutions are ideas. Solutions are alternative strategies. Solutions to problems answer the question: "How can I (we) make it happen?" The it refers to the desired end result.

When solutions get institutionalized in a society they become bodies of knowledge. For example, what is medicine? It is the collection of solutions to the problem of illness that experts have deemed appropriate. What is education? Experts have codified the solutions to the problem of socializing the young (and those older) and preparing them for a role in society. As you run through college curricula you will find that each body of knowledge represents the prevailing solutions in that discipline.

What distinguishes a university, ideally, is that it employs scholars whose job it is to discover new solutions to problems. However, in many universities, as well as in colleges, high schools and grade schools throughout the land, practitioners fall in love with the solutions they learned and mastered and do not want to entertain new ways of doing things.

This is true not only in the educational arena, where there is pervasive conflict between the old ways and the new ways, but everywhere else—between the older generation and the newer generation; between the creator and the consumer; between the radical and the conservative, between the free spirit and the true believer.

When people fall in love with their solutions and impose them on others, the desirable virtue becomes obedience; obedience to the solutions that prevail. Obedience is a useful virtue, but what happens in business and in our schools is that it typically becomes the dominant virtue. Little premium is put on creativity, problem solving, or improvement. Questioning the status quo is anathema, simply not done.

CULTURE AS A SET OF SOLUTIONS

When we look at societies on a macro scale we know that for them to survive, they must solve fundamental survival problems, e.g., develop food sources, find shelter, have a governing system, ensure justice, educate the young, and the like. All of the solutions that a society comes up with in the aggregate constitute that society's culture. So a culture could be defined as the answers, the solutions to problems, that a group agrees work.

The problem with solutions is that one person's, group's, or society's solutions often become some other person's, group's, or society's problems. Thus, we are left with a terrible fact of life—solutions cause problems. Therefore, whatever solutions we come up with are tentative answers. We need to understand and accept that there is no steady state, no Shangri-la, no Nirvana, no heaven on earth. Like death, taxes and the poor, problems will always be with us. We need problems to become motivated, to take on the challenge of solving problems as a positive, as a way of life, and the source from which joy can flow.

HOW TO DEEPEN MOTIVATION TO SOLVE A PROBLEM

Sometimes we have problems and yet procrastinate about solving them, or simply ignore them. We discover that they usually don't go away and, in many cases, worsen. But often, even with the acute awareness that we need to deal with a problem, we find it difficult to move into a problem-solving mode. What can we do about it?

First, it is important to understand that there are only two things that motivate a person to do anything—reward or pain. People will act to obtain reward from the action or to avoid the pain they will experience if they don't act. Strangely enough, people will do more to avoid pain than to reap the positive reward that flows from a course of action.

Knowing this, how can we motivate ourselves to get on with solving a problem when we are confronted with one? It is very simple:

1. Get a blank sheet of paper and write the problem across the top.
2. Draw a line down the middle of the page.
3. In the left column write, "Rewards—if I solve it."
4. In the right column write, "Pains—if I don't solve it."
5. Next list as many of the rewards and pains as you can think of in the appropriate column.

When done, step back, reflect on what you wrote down. If what you wrote does not move you into action, I don't know what else will.

APPLICATION TO SELF

So, how can you use this simple exercise? Whenever you are dealing with a problem, even if you already are enthusiastic about solving it, take the time to delineate your payoffs—the rewards you will reap and the pains you will avoid when you do indeed solve the problem. You will find that your motivation will deepen, and your commitment to completing the task will become unshakable.

THE GREATEST SKILL OF ALL

It is the contention here that the greatest skill of all is problem solving. It is at the root of invention, progress, improvement, enrichment, and fulfillment. Once you master the contents of this book and become a master problem solver, beware, your life will never be the same. You will become a gadfly; you will ask questions all the time; you will challenge the *status quo*; you will make others uncomfortable. So, unless you are financially independent, do not abandon common sense in your challenges—please be prudent. However, in the process of unleashing your creative potential, you will become more fully alive, more enthusiastic about your life and work and more enriched by the heights to which you will have risen and the stories you will be able to tell.

Incidentally, to master this book, read it five times.

CHAPTER 4

HOW TO GET INTO A RESOURCEFUL STATE ON DEMAND

How You Feel Will Dictate What You Do

"In order to achieve or realise his natural unity with his universe, man must first attain unity within himself—by balancing body, mind, and emotions."

—Dan Millman

Have you ever tried to balance your checkbook after an argument with your spouse? Have you ever had the "blahs"" and felt unable to get it together? Have you ever felt dissipated and simply could not focus? Were you ever in a blue funk and found yourself gazing into space? Have you ever felt overwhelmed, or hassled, or inundated by the demands confronting you? Have you ever had a pile of things to do and yet could only stare at the pile? Have you ever had a serious problem and did not even know where to begin?

If you answered "yes" to one of the above questions, it means that at that point you found yourself in an unresourceful state. Folks in an unresourceful state simply do not have the creative problem-solving part of their brain available to them. As a consequence, they cannot make a decision, they wind up in neutral, time gets wasted, and usually the problem gets worse.

An unresourceful state is a "feel bad" state—the specific feeling could be depression, anger, sadness, disappointment, loss, guilt, worry, fear, or the like. In some respects, which feeling it is does not matter because the consequence is the same—it puts a person into an unresourceful state; they are simply not in the mood to solve a problem and, as a consequence, either do not try, or proceed only with a great struggle.

THE BIG QUESTION

So, the big question is "how can a person get into a resourceful state?" There are four elements that can accelerate the process, one of which I dealt with in the previous chapters, i.e., proper attitude. Without the appropriate mind set, solving problems can be an uphill march with a 90-pound pack on your back. By getting this far in this book, it shows you are moving in the right direction and, by embracing the beliefs I suggested about reality, change, and problems, you are galloping ahead.

The other three keys to fine tuning your instrument are:

1. Achieve high energy
2. Get centered
3. Anchor yourself

ACHIEVE HIGH ENERGY

Why is it important for a problem solver to have a high level of energy? A high level of energy helps a person to feel good physically. High energy, further, leads to good health. Being healthy and feeling good physically is like having a well-tuned violin that is ready to play. It is an essential condition to playing beautiful music and an essential condition to maximize creative expression.

The reverse is also true when a violinist picks up his instrument and the strings are broken and out of tune; his chances of producing any art are zero. Likewise when a problem solver has low energy and is sick, the desire to solve anything evaporates and, in serious cases of illness, the person might just want to hide under the covers. Even if a person is not sick, and just has low energy, patience goes, and the ability to sustain any degree of creative thinking erodes profoundly. As a consequence, the first solution that comes to mind is accepted and execution is often inadequate.

So, if you want to play beautiful music, tune the violin. If you want to drive your car, fill your tank, and if you want to prepare yourself to be a dynamic problem solver, be a high-energy person.

HOW DO YOU BECOME A HIGH ENERGY PROBLEM SOLVER?

There are four dimensions to achieving sustained high energy: breathing properly, eating properly, moving properly, and knowing how to relax.

Breathing

Since you have to breathe anyway, you might as well breathe properly. Two things can be done:

1. Regular diaphragmatic, or "belly breathing."
2. Three times a day take ten deep breaths in the following manner:
   a. Inhale through the nose for the count of five.
   b. Drive the breath down to your lower abdomen and let it balloon up.
   c. Hold the breath for the count of 20.
   d. Exhale slowly out through your mouth for the count of ten.

Notice the ratio: 5, 20, 10 = 1, 4, 2. You can take a deeper and longer inhalation, e.g., 6 inhale, 24 hold, 12 exhale. This exercise can be done in meetings, driving, waiting, in airplanes, bed, office, etc.

When you do deep breathing regularly, as indicated, the cobwebs in the brain disappear, and your intellectual alertness improves demonstrably.

Eating

Forget about dieting, and do three things:

1. Make 70% of what you eat water-content foods—fruits and vegetables.

2. Fall in love with whole grains.

3. Keep your fat intake as low as possible. If you are regularly eating well-balanced meals, i.e., fruit, vegetables, whole grains, fish and fowl, you will get all the dietary fat your body needs.

Moving

The key to fitness and high energy is aerobic exercise.

However, there is an important caution: If you are physically unfit, and have not exercised much beside power lifting a knife and fork, check with your physician to make sure you are not a candidate for a heart attack before you start your aerobic exercise program. Intensive care really crimps your zest for problem solving.

1. The rule of thumb is simple: As a minimum, do 12 minutes of continuous aerobic exercise every day in your Training Zone.

a. What is the Training Zone?

It is where all good things happen to your body, e.g., production of fat-burning enzymes. It can vary, but for the majority of folks it equals 65 to 80% of your maximum heart rate.

b. How do you get to know your maximum heart rate? Although it can vary, a rule of thumb for the majority of people is: 220 minus your age.

c. How do you figure out your Training Zone?

Suppose your age is 30; 220 minus 30 = 190—the maximum heart rate for a thirty year old. Sixty-five percent of 190 = 124, the lower level of your training zone; eighty percent of 190 = 152, the upper limit of your training zone. If you are 30 years of age, (although it can vary), for the majority of folks that age, the training zone equals 124 to 152 beats per minute. Figure it out for your age using this example as a guide.

d. How do you get into the Training Zone?

Warm up by doing a slower version of the aerobic exercise for about three minutes.

e. How do you know when you are beyond the Training Zone?

Do the "talk test"—if you can say "God Bless America, Land That I Love" (or the first seven words from your national anthem) without gasping for air, you are not beyond the Training Zone.

f. How can you avoid boredom?

Vary the type of aerobic exercise from one day to the next. Remember there is a lot to choose from, so choose ones that are enjoyable, e.g., walking, brisk walking, jogging, swimming, biking, cross-country skiing, stationary bicycling, rowing, stair climbing, bench stepping, jumping rope, treadmill, mini-trampoline, aerobic dancing, and mowing your lawn with a push mower.

2. Based on the above, what is a minimalist aerobic exercise program?

A minimalist aerobic exercise program would be: fifteen minutes a day—three minutes warm-up and 12 minutes of continuous aerobic exercise in your training zone.

If you can do more exercise within your training zone, that is even better.

Rewards

The payoffs for this regimen of breathing, eating, and exercise are colossal: Energy is up, health improves, longevity increases, self-esteem grows, tension is relieved, muscles become toned, obesity disappears, appearance improves and, above all, your problem-solving capability becomes finely tuned.

THE BODY AND THE MIND

A focus on the physical can indeed make us better problem solvers. However, we need to find a way to focus our mind.

But first, what unfocuses us? The experience of stress, when unchecked, can lead to high blood pressure, a range of psychosomatic illnesses, and can profoundly erode our problem-solving capability. The physical regimen previously described can directly alleviate much of the distress we experience in our lives. But regularly bringing on the "relaxation response" is an even more powerful technique for winding down the body, feeling centered, and achieving serenity. Why? Because the "relaxation response" leads to deep relaxation and deep relaxation is the most important precondition for relieving stress and experiencing a sense of peace and wholeness. In this state our problem-solving aptitude is at its zenith.

THE METHOD FOR BRINGING ON THE RELAXATION RESPONSE

1. Choose two euphonious (nice sounding) syllables and put them together to form a two-syllable sound. This will be your focus vehicle. It will give your active mind something to do while your body is winding down; for example; *ab ba; se la; oh mo; I an*, etc. Make one up for yourself.
2. Sitting in a comfortable position, with eyes closed, think the nonsense sound, your focus vehicle, over and over and over—slowly, fluidly, rhythmically.
3. After 15 to 20 minutes stop your sound, keep your eyes closed, and for one to two minutes think about the problem for which you are seeking solutions. At the end of this period open your eyes and move into action.
4. An ideal use of the "relaxation response" is twice each day—once in early morning before breakfast and your exercise regimen; and then again before dinner.

However, remember something is better than nothing! If you cannot do it twice a day, do it once. If you cannot do it for 15 to 20 minutes, do ten, or five, or even two minutes. If you cannot find two minutes of quiet time for yourself, you are in trouble.

5. Do the "relaxation response" sitting up in bed, in the office, airline terminals, doctor's office, or wherever you have to wait. As with deep breathing, you always have something valuable to do with down time.

The Rewards

Besides allowing you to be enthusiastic about solving your problems, the "relaxation response" increases the feelings of peace, winds down the body, reframes your perspective, lowers blood pressure, increases energy, and gives the body a chance to repair itself.

PUTTING YOURSELF INTO A PROBLEM-SOLVING MOOD

Have you ever noticed that often when you have a problem, that you simply are not in the mood to deal with it? Well, there is an intimate connection between how you feel at a given moment and whether you have the internal motivation to get on with business. So, if you want to make your problem-solving capabilities more available to yourself, it is important to be in a "feel good" state. When you "feel good" you are at your most resourceful, and your chances of solving your problems are greater.

HOW DO YOU GET INTO A "FEEL GOOD" STATE?

The way you can do this is by conditioning yourself. It is analogous to the way Pavlov conditioned his dog. He would show his dog meat, the dog would salivate, and Pavlov would ring a bell. He kept repeating the process, until after a while all he had to do to make the dog salivate was to ring the bell. You can do something similar, except we call it anchoring, and you do it for yourself and by yourself to move into a life-enhancing "feel good" state.

Anchoring

To create a positive anchor, do the following:

1. Choose an emotion that you would like to have at your fingertips that makes you "feel good"—e.g., enthusiasm.

2. Take yourself back in your mind to a time when you really felt that way, for instance, when you received your last promotion, or something else that filled you with enthusiasm.

3. Link that feeling with a gesture and a sound, such as making a fist and saying "yes!"

4. While holding the experience in your mind and feeling the emotion, repeat the trigger (the gesture and word) five times. For most people this will fix the anchor. If it does not, do it five more times, or until it works.

5. The real test of whether the feeling (enthusiasm) is anchored, is to test the anchor a few hours later, or the next day, and observe the transformation of your state. If it does not move you into your desired state, go back and retrace step number 1; make the emotion more intense, and the experience more vivid in your imagination. Then trip the trigger at the peak of that feeling again and again—five times. This should do it.

YOUR PROBLEM-SOLVING INSTRUMENT

Now you know how to keep your body and mind fine tuned. If you follow the simple regimen outlined above with consistency, you will discover that not only will your problem-solving acuity be improved significantly, but also the entire quality of your life.

COUNTING LEADS TO CONTROL

The best way to control behavior and to instill new habits is to count your successes. So, make a grid for a month at a time, and put an X in the box each time you do one of the four elements that can condition you, the problem solver.

	1	2	3	4	5	6	7	8	9	10	11	etc.
Deep Breathing (10 x 3x)												
Eating (70/30)												
Moving (15 minutes)												
Relaxation (20 minutes 2x)												

Figure 1: Control Grid

DO IT NOW!

CHAPTER 5

MAKE A QUESTION OF EVERYTHING

The Power of Inquisitiveness

"Ask, and you will receive...."

—Matthew 7.7

T he quickest and most direct way to stimulate creativity is to ask questions. A question is provocative; it stimulates, prods, and stretches. A question, by its nature, demands an answer. A questioner is unsettled, discontent and searching for something other than what he has. On the other hand, when a person makes a statement and puts a period at the end of it, that's it! Nothing needs to follow to get closure on the thought. Periods do not provoke; judgments do not open the mind; question marks do.

BECOME A CHILD AGAIN

All we need to do to recover our tremendous creativity is to become a child again. A child who has not been discouraged searches for knowledge, for understanding. What is a child's favorite word? Why!

Why do birds fly? Why do dogs bark? Why do we use money? Why does my boat float? Why do we tell time? Why do people speak different languages? A child has other provokers as well—Where does the sun go at night? Who is Uncle Buddy? When is my program coming on? Or, what's that? Or, how come?

The child is searching for information to satisfy the innate longing to understand the world. Often adults respond to these queries by an attack, by sarcasm, by silence, by ridicule. When this occurs, after awhile, the child stops asking questions and creativity goes underground.

Regardless of what has happened to you in the past, give yourself permission to be a questioner and make it a strong part of your approach to life. You will find your creativity will charge out of the castle when the drawbridge is let down. Let the child in you come out.

THE RIGHT KIND OF QUESTIONS—EMPOWERING ONES

In Chapter 1 you were exposed to disempowering questions—endless loop questions and wrong questions. What are empowering questions? They are questions that open the mind, that search honestly for information or alternatives and flow out of genuine curiosity. They are a sincere search for solutions or adventure.

But how do you formulate a question? That's easy. Simply put a question mark after anything and preface it by: who, what, where, when, why, how. For example, I am sitting on my couch right now looking at a vase. Using the "vase" as the object of inquiry, ask:

Who made the vase?
Where did the vase come from?
When was the vase put on the coffee table?
What material is the vase made of?
Why was this vase chosen?
How was the vase sold?

If you dissect the previous questions, there are four parts:

The interrogative: who, what, where, why, when, how;
The object of inquiry: the vase;

Attributes of the vase: design, cost, materials, and the like;

A verb: bought, made, put, chosen, sold, come from.

Because the number of verbs is virtually unlimited and the number of attributes we could explore about the vase is vast, e.g.:

The design of the vase;
the weight of the vase;
the cost of the vase;
the meaning of the vase;
the shape of the vase;
the creation of the vase;
the inspiration for the vase;

the number of questions we could ask about the vase could fill this entire book. What we do not know about the vase is awesome. So, what do questions do? They provoke a search—a search for knowledge, a search for understanding. Questions thus become the vehicle to quench the thirst to know. Why? Think of the reverse— no questions, no provocation, no stimulation, no forward momentum, no inquiry, no search. We are left with a vapid confrontation with what is—and if that is a person's orientation, they will be bored and will be boring to others.

A person who is bored asks no questions. Questions are what get our wheels spinning, our hearts racing, and enthusiasm ignited. A person who does not question is a sheep, is led by someone who has the answer. In totalitarian organizations members are not allowed to ask questions. The absence of questions is thus the key to disempowerment and, ultimately, to slavery.

Questions, on the other hand, lead to *perestroika*. They provoke answers; the more questions, the more answers and pretty soon folks start deviating from the party line. So questions can be dangerous to the *status quo*. Questions cause disequilibrium and are at the root of cultural change, innovation, exploration, creativity, science and, of course, problem solving. Questions are, in a word, empowering because they thrust the questioner forward into new and uncharted waters.

WHAT DO WE NEED TO BE AN ASKER/A QUESTIONER?

We need to accept the biblical axiom "ask and you will receive." If you do not ask, you will not receive, and you will wind up with more of the same. When we do ask, we will receive. What? New ideas, new thoughts, new possibilities, new alternatives. So, if we have a problem, what we need to realize is that we do not have a money problem, a customer-dissatisfaction problem, a child problem, a motivation problem, a communication problem. What we have is an "idea problem" and, more to the point, a "lack of ideas problem" with respect to money, customer dissatisfaction, children, motivation, or communication. The prime way to solve the problem is to ask questions because the answers to those questions will generate ideas and solutions.

MORE IS BEST

The key to coming up with a great idea, a quality idea, as mentioned earlier, is to have a lot of ideas that are possible. From there we can select the one that is the most promising. For example, suppose you had a beauty contest and only one woman showed up; suppose you organized a marathon and only one runner ran; suppose you were a director auditioning actors for a key role and one person came to the audition. In each instance you would feel compromised, and that you were stuck with what you had. That's exactly what happens, so often, when people are trying to solve problems: the first idea that comes to their mind is the last. Unfortunately, they often do not feel compromised and usually go with that solution, oblivious to better possibilities. That is why there is so much mediocrity; people get wedded to their way, albeit inferior, and do not want to entertain anything else. Thus, ugly gets chosen, a slow runner wins, and miscasting occurs.

The key is to have a lot of ideas and the way to generate a lot of ideas is to have a lot of questions. To save time in figuring out your own questions (which I encourage you to do) following you will find *The Option Generator*. It is a series of questions you can bring to bear on any problem. The way to use it is simple:

1. With a problem in mind, such as "How could I increase sales volume?," Ask the question, and wait; listen to your inner voice respond. Imagine you have an incredible data bank in your head and that you have a little man up there waiting to rifle through the file cabinets and to come up with a possibility. All he needs to start his search is a question. So, ask him the questions.

2. Get a pencil and paper and capture any idea or idea fragment that comes to your mind.

3. Proceed slowly through all 108 questions in The Option Generator—pretty soon you will have a pageful of possibilities.

4. Notice the questions are broken into categories. There is nothing precious about these categories—they simply point the direction of the subsequent questions.

5. You will notice that some of the questions might not fit your particular problem. No problem. Just move ahead—most of the questions will stimulate something.

THE OPTION GENERATOR

The Questions

NB. In business, solutions to problems almost always require a team effort. That is why "we" is the personal pronoun in the question. When you are, indeed, working on a personal problem, substitute "I" for "we."

Adapt

How can we use something that works elsewhere?
What can we copy? Or imitate?
What might be suitable if modified?
How have others solved this or similar problems? Our vendors? Our customers? Our competitors?
How would people in other disciplines solve it? Cultures?
How can we turn our problem into an opportunity?
What two or more things, if joined, would make something new?
  People? Products? Technologies? Services? Materials? Functions? Organizations? Inventions?

Streamline

In what way can we make the process leaner? Smoother?
How can we make it more responsive? More direct?
What are the "precious" things that have outlived their usefulness?
What can be eliminated?
What can be compressed? Or by-passed?
What can be ignored?
What one format can be used with many variations?
How can we make our service/product more appealing?
How can we achieve and keep high levels of customer satisfaction?
How can the frequency of customized or special products be reduced? Or increased?
How can we use an express line? Do more with less?

Reorganize

In what ways can the elements be set up differently?
How can they be rearranged? Rescheduled?
How can we alter established priorities?

Can we start at the end?
Can we do just the opposite?
Can the way to solve this problem begin from the inside out?
How can we rotate the elements?
What could be a surprise or unexpected result?
What other materials can be used? Procedures? Processes?
  Markets? Technologies? Suppliers? Locations? Persons?
What new targets can we establish?

Change

In what ways can we speed up?
How can we magnify our impact?
In what ways can we add value to other functions?
How can we multiply the number of positive ripples we send out?
How can we put more sizzle into what we're selling? Get more visibility?
In what ways can we raise quality?
How can we achieve zero defects?
How can we give customers more than they expect?
Are there obstacles we can remove? Minimize?
Are there things that can be reduced? Made smaller? Condensed?
Would it make any sense to slow down?
Are there things we can subtract? Divide? Break up?
How can we lower the cost?
How can we decrease response time? Shorten intervals?
How can we lessen customer complaints?
How can we help those we serve become more successful?

What Else?

What else could *it* be used for?
Are there new markets for our services? Products?

Suppose our capability was portable? Mobile?
Does our expertise suggest any spin-offs? In other fields?
What needs exist in the marketplace that our skill could address? For individuals? Families? Organizations? Others?
How can we enrich the lives of our associates with our capability?
How can we change the meaning of what we do?
    The setting? The attitudes and habits of those on board?
How can we alter the reward system? Change policy?
How can we use time more effectively?
How can we differentiate our function? Distinguish it?
How can we alter perceptions of others and persuade them great things are happening?
How can we improve what we do?
How can we get colleagues to feel they are a part of the team?

Paradoxical Thinking

Remember, we are looking for inspiration; so do not be misled by the following questions. We want you to draw some positive thoughts out of considering the opposite scenarios.
How can we worsen an already difficult situation?
How can we snatch defeat from the jaws of victory?
How can we close this window of opportunity?
How can we let things slip through the cracks?
How can we really get cemented into our present position?
What can we do to make the losses greater?

What If...Scenarios

What if we discover a new way?
What if we blithely ignore the problem?
What if we accept the first solution that pops into mind?
What if we take a very conservative posture?
What if we try...?

RESULTS—IDEAS WITH TEETH

When you are done, what do you do? You have a myriad of possibilities. Now go back over your possibilities, and add, subtract, or modify the statements as written. Next you will want to make the ideas more precise. Go back over your list and reformulate any idea that looks somewhat promising in the following way:

"To do how much of what by when."

For example, suppose one of your thoughts to improve profitable sales volume was "revisit old customers." The way to make this precise would be: "Revisit all old customers (last three years) by the end of the year."

Or, suppose another idea was: "to create show room events." Put more precisely, it would be: "To invite 500 prospects to five meaningful showroom events by year's end."

These are what I call ideas with "teeth." This sharpening of your statement creates actionable ideas. What are actionable ideas? They are ideas about which you can do something. Actionable ideas precede decision making and decision making leads to action, and action leads to results. Results are the name of the game.

ASSIGNMENT

Copy the questions in the option generator, and keep them nearby when you are looking for ideas. Use all the questions, if you have the time, as you work through a problem or use only some of them in a modified application. But keep them at hand, visible, and be acutely aware that he or she who "asks will receive."

CHAPTER 6

HOW TO DO MIND MAPPING

*Pictures Produce
Possibilities*

"One picture is worth a thousand words."

—Chinese Proverb

You now understand the power of questions and the importance of a questioning orientation. In this chapter this mind set will be linked to a more visual stimulus.

Put yourself into a resourceful state, and let's begin. A way that works for me is the following:

Imagine your brain is a dump truck and that it has inside of it a vast collection of diverse, disconnected, pieces of information. If I unload a dump truck, I raise the release lever and the dirt comes tumbling out. Once the dirt is out on the ground I can allocate portions of it to areas at the building site. Likewise with the brain, if I get the information/data dumped out first, then I can sort through it and figure out what goes where, which comes first, and what do I do next.

The best way for me to do a data dump is to develop a mind map. A mind map is fun because it generates a visual picture of the flotsam and jetsam inside your head. It is easy to do because it requires little exercise of judgment, no evaluation, and is much like capturing your stream of consciousness.

THE RELEASE LEVER—THE FOCUS QUESTION

However, to complicate things a little, imagine your brain is the garage, not for just one dump truck and its cargo, but for a thousand dump trucks and their cargos. The first thing we have to do is to select which dump truck we want to dump. We do this by formulating a focus question—the focus question ignores all the other dump trucks and selects one. If I have a problem; it is about something, e.g., money, customers, relationships, goals, and the like. A focus question takes that "something" and simply puts it in the form of a question, for example "what can I do about…?" The question thus ignores all other dump trucks, focuses on the one, and becomes the release lever that allows the ideas to spill out.

HOW TO DO IT

The way to do it is simple. In the middle of a blank page write a question. Suppose my challenge is to write a book on problem solving. What would a dump look like using a mind map? See *Figure 2*.

Notice the focus question in the circle: "Where do I begin my book on problem solving?" Ideas popped randomly into my mind and I simply drew a balloon around the thought and a string connecting it to the core. When that idea suggested other ideas, such as "catalog techniques," I drew balloons around each separate thought and connected each with a string back to "catalog techniques"—i.e., mind maps, questions, beliefs, and Quantum Leap Thinking. The key to doing this fruitfully is to suspend your judgment.

SUSPEND YOUR JUDGMENT

What does suspend your judgment mean? It means do not evaluate it or weigh whether the thought is good or bad or whether it is perfectly expressed or not. Just get it out and on paper even if it is only a thought fragment.

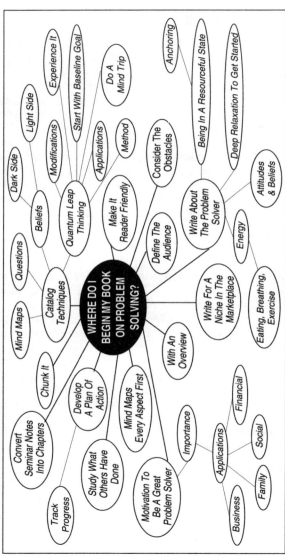

Figure 2:
Mind Map of My Book On Problem Solving

The second propelling thought in creativity is to go for quantity. Anything can stimulate an idea; so the more thoughts you have out there, the more other thoughts they will stimulate. It is almost like a geometric progression where you go from 1 to 2, to 4, to 8. Working off of a focus question, you can literally fill up a page with a plethora of ideas quickly. And the beauty of all this is that, by having a lot of ideas you increase the chances of coming up with a quality idea(s).

QUESTION MARKS

A provocative way to generate a lot of thoughts is to simply put a question mark after any category you write down. The question mark symbolizes: "What about it?" When combined with the classic interrogatives, who, what, where, why, when, and how, the responses spawn so many thoughts that the hard part is capturing them. Notice the example below, where I simply follow one thought from the previous mind map in *Figure 2*, i.e., "catalog techniques."

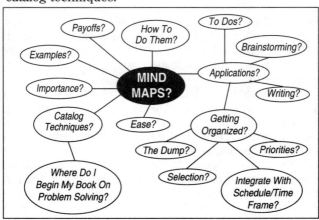

Figure 3:
Part of a Mind Map—Amplifying One Thought

You will notice in *Figure 2* the actual question marks were not drawn in, whereas in *Figure 3*, they were. This is simply to give you a choice in terms of graphic presentation. What is important though is that, even where the questions marks are not actually drawn, they should exist in your mind and imagination. Transforming every category, or thought fragment into a question propels and propagates more thoughts and ideas. As mentioned earlier, questions push, stimulate, provoke, unlock, amplify, and expand the range of considerations. Since quantity is the key to quality, mind mapping from a questioning perspective is a primary tool in finding creative solutions because it combines power questions with a visual unfolding of what develops.

AN EXERCISE FOR PRACTICE

Here is an exercise for you: Write out a focus question in the middle of a blank sheet of paper and put a circle around it. With one eye on the example provided in *Figure 2* allow your subconscious mind to offer up ideas. Wait. As each one bubbles up to the surface, capture it with a balloon and a string. When you are dry, simply go back to the focus question, and ask it again; wait; then capture.

If you want to expand on any balloon, simply put a question mark after it, e.g., when I put "Quantum Leap Thinking" out there, I asked myself: "What could I say about Quantum Leap Thinking?" Notice the responses—method, applications, experience it, modifications, start with the baseline goal, doing a mind trip. Any of these categories could be expanded in a like manner. So, formulate a focus question for some practice. Take something that is troubling you, or something that needs improvement, or choose one of the focus questions below and play with it:

Sample Focus Questions

How can we improve profitability?
How can we motivate our people better?
What are the ways we can improve market share?
How can we truly dazzle our customers?
How can we make it easy to cross-sell?
How can we become the product of choice?
How can we improve cycle time?
What can we do to double throughput?
What need can we meet that is presently unmet?
What cost reductions have we overlooked?
How can we become known without paid advertising?
What new ways can we go to market?
How can we sell value and not just price?
Where are our opportunities?
What are the things our competitors are not doing?
How can we crunch product development?
How can we become known for quality?
Where can we get financing?
Where are all the good men/women?
How can I surround myself with outstanding people?
What is the image we want to send to the market place?
Where can I find outstanding minorities?
How can we distribute this product?
Are there services we could add to this product?
How can we keep our people focused?
What can we do about health care costs?
How can we make our suppliers as good as we are?

These are only a small sample of the kind of focus question a businessman might ask himself. Choose one, or make one up of your own choosing and mind map your responses.

HOW ELSE CAN MIND MAPS BE USED?

To answer this question let us start with a mind map.

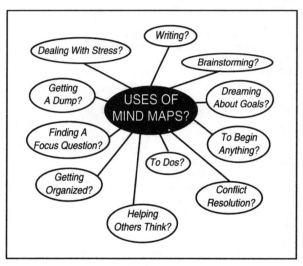

Figure 4:
Mind Map Applications

The uses of mind maps are numerous. Virtually anytime you are in a search mode, pondering alternatives, or trying to get started on a project, you will find mind maps get you started quickly. For example, anytime I have to write a chapter, or even a segment of a chapter, I stop and do a mind map. It gets the dump out there, and puts me in a position to choose, select and delete, just as I am doing right now with this segment of the chapter.

TO DOS

One of my favorite ways to use a mind map is with my daily **TO DOs**. I simply draw a circle in the middle of a blank sheet of paper, and inside I put: **TO DO?** Then I dump out all the things I must do, could do, and will do on that day. Once they are out there, I plug them into a time frame that I have on the right. See *Figure 5* for a copy of a blank mind map **"TO DO"** format.

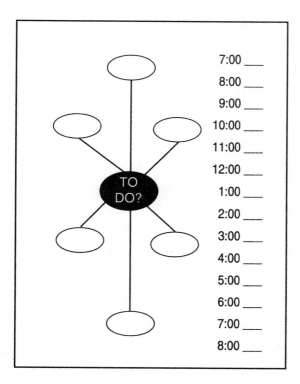

Figure 5:
"To Do" Blank Mind Map With Time Frame

As you can see from the earlier mind map in *Figure 4* on page 58, there are many other applications of mind maps. In Chapter 11, I will show you how to use one when you are overwhelmed with problems. The idea is to test it out; maybe you too will become addicted to them. They are a great tool to help unleash creativity.

CHAPTER 7

ASSOCIATION AND FISHHOOKING

Inspiration is Everywhere

"When the wind is in the East,
Then the fishes bite the least;
When the wind is in the West,
Then the fishes bite the best;
When the wind is in the North,
Then the fishes do come forth;
When the wind is in the South,
It blows the bait in the fish's mouth."

—Anonymous

So far, two powerful techniques for becoming a creative problem solver have been explained: 1) Questioning, and 2) Mind Mapping. If you regularly use either of them your creativity already will show signs of exploding. But more is in store for you. In this chapter the focus will be on association. Once you understand the principle of association and put it into practice, you will find yourself on the express line to problem solving, and never be at a loss for possibilities.

THE PRINCIPLE OF ASSOCIATION

The principle of association relates to the way your memory works. Inside your brain you have billions of pieces of data. Everything you ever read, observed, felt, smelled, touched, heard, or even thought is floating around inside your brain. The depth and breadth of this library in your brain is simply prodigious. Our basic problem is getting access to this font of knowledge and using it to help solve our problems.

AN EXERCISE IN IMAGINATION

A way to help explain the principle is to imagine that your brain is a huge lake filled with fish. The fish represent bits of data. In order to catch a fish, it is necessary to throw a hook into the water. When the hook is thrown in, because of the density of the fish, you, the fisherman, will pull something out. Now the interesting thing when you are fishing for ideas is that *anything* can be a hook. Anything can catch a fish—we just need to take the initiative to throw the hook in. What this means in problem solving is that *anything* can be the source of inspiration for something new, different, exciting, productive, or effective.

Let us suppose we already have identified our problem. For example: "How can we sell one million tires by year's end?" Now, what we are searching for are possible ways to achieve the goal. The near-term objective of the exercise is to generate many ideas, on the principle that if you have a lot of ideas your chances of coming up with a quality idea increase.

RANDOM LISTS OF CONCRETE WORDS

Step one is to make a random list of concrete things that have nothing to do with marketing tires. These will become the fishhooks. We will then see what they might catch that could have some bearing on selling a million tires.

List Of Words

> ants
> chair
> alarm clock
> ice pop
> bubonic plague

Step two is to look at "ants." In a playful manner think about ants: Who they are, what they do, where they live, how they behave, and why they behave the way they do. Ask yourself intermittently, how could this help me sell a million tires? For example:

Ants?   Ants are small; a lot of customers feel small, ignorant, intimidated because they have little knowledge of tires. Educate them first, sell them second.

There are trillions of ants—all sizes and shapes; understand the enormity of my market and stratify it by important factors, e.g., age, gender, ethnic background. Make it easy for each class to do business with us. There is not one message we need to develop but rather a variety.

When we learn about ants, we begin to value and appreciate them. We need to learn about our customers and appreciate them. Teach salesman to regard them kindly, not as an inconvenience, or the enemy—and to listen to them.

Chair?   Put chairs around the showroom to make customers comfortable.

Make something new out of old tires; a chair out of tires. Promote creative uses for recycling tires—display of tire planters; shelves; shoes; play ground; tables; toys; art objects; boat bumpers; fences, and the like.

For each set of four tires, we give free a tire swing—the only thing that will cost anything is the rope.

Alarm clock?   Give salespeople a deadline to hit quotas. Give customers an eight-hour sale that ends when the alarm goes off.

Wake up calls to customers—maybe we could try telemarketing and sell tires by phone.

Ice pop? Run a super special snow tire sale in July—this would be out of the ordinary. Make it a layaway.

Give away free ice pops to anyone who walks into the showroom. As traffic goes up, sales will go up.

Have a huge ice sculpture of a tire made, and have a contest: Give a free set of tires to the person who guesses how many gallons of water it contains.

Bubonic plague? Auto accidents are a horrible plague—promote safety, security, and our no-failure record.

Mount an ad campaign likening Edgar Allan Poe's *The Masque of the Red Death* to riding around on bald tires, where the driver and others could be injured.

Promote the idea that the cure for fear, worry, anxiety, on the road is our most advanced and reliable tire.

Let us find a way to make our good deals contagious so satisfied customers will send other customers—maybe a $10 reward for every referral that ends in a sale. Make every customer a commissioned salesperson.

Now notice what we did with the five randomly selected concrete words. They were the fishhooks and what did they pull out—17 ideas; and many of them are great ideas, e.g., hassle-free customer service; educate the consumer; importance of market niches; ideas for building traffic into the showroom—displays, contests, deadlines; new ways of selling, such as telemarketing, using fear motivation, and making every customer a commissioned salesperson. And remember, all you need to solve most problems is one good idea.

You can do the same: Formulate your problem in terms of a question; write out a random list of concrete words and even make some of them weird or bizarre. Then, with your problem in mind, reflect on what each word might suggest that could help solve your problem. Incidentally, this is fun when you do it alone, but is even more fun when you do it with a group.

A WEIRDER EXERCISE

If one column of randomly selected words can be so productive, what about two columns? With the following exercise, you will see for yourself.

1. List five concrete words on the left side of a sheet of paper.
2. List five concrete words on the right.
3. Draw a line from a word in the left column to any word on the right.
4. Do likewise for every other left column word.
5. With the two words coupled, ask yourself what ideas they might suggest to solve your problem.

Let us use the same problem as before: "How can we sell one million tires by year end?"

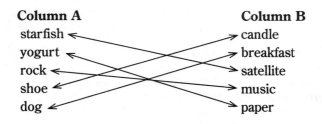

Column A	Column B
starfish	candle
yogurt	breakfast
rock	satellite
shoe	music
dog	paper

Now look at the pairs:

> starfish satellite
> yogurt paper
> rock music
> shoe candle
> dog breakfast

Take each set and ask what it suggests that would help sell one million tires.

Starfish satellite? Set fireworks, starbursts off each night for a week to attract attention to a tire sale.

Organize a nationwide network for selling tires similar to the way mattresses are sold.

Yogurt paper? Advertise in newspapers and give away free frozen yogurt to anyone who visits the showroom.

Slice a thin segment of the market, the yogurt/granola crowd, and give it a special pitch for upscale tires.

Rock music? Give out musical pet rocks for every sale.

Advertise in rock n' roll print media.

Create a rock music/rap jingle about our great tires.

Shoe candle? Do a series of tire torture tests—kicking the tires with a mule; resisting a flame thrower, and the like.

Combine it with G. Gordon Liddy and his famous hand-over-the-candle test, as well as from the lady villain kicking a tire from the James Bond movie with the knife in her shoe tip.

Sell tires door to door—in the evening.

Dog breakfast?   Have a special pet owners tie-in with tires and dog food.

Be dogged about having customers coming in and "have breakfast on us."

Now look at some of those ideas. Not all are knockouts, but some have merit. When you do this exercise, you find that some combinations of words leave you bone dry—no inspiration. In that case, just pass over them and move on to the next one. We do not need to beat a starfish satellite to death. If it does not come fast and does not come easy, please don't sweat it. It simply means you should move on and try another hook.

Again, although it is fun doing this exercise alone, it borders on hilarious when you do it with a group. It helps everyone to get into a playful childlike mood. And you will be surprised—frequently some great ideas jump out that you would not have thought of otherwise. Remember our refrain: How many good ideas do you need to solve your problem?

YELLOW PAGES AS THE FISHHOOK

Suppose you have a problem. You are thinking about going into business, but are not sure what kind of business would make sense. Since you know that so many inventions occur as a consequence of combining two things that exist independently, you decide to look in the Yellow Pages for possibilities.

Try this exercise with the Yellow Pages. Make an association grid by listing ten categories from the Yellow Pages; then run them side by side along the top axis. This generates a grid—we can then speculate how any of the boxes might generate an opportunity for business that no one is providing. See *Figure 6*.

Now look at the combinations and see what they

	Auto	Books	Carpet	Dentists	Employment	Fire	Glass	Hardware	Insurance	Janitor
Automobile										
Books										
Carpet										
Dentists										
Employment										
Fire										
Glass										
Hardware										
Insurance										
Janitor										

Figure 6:
Yellow Pages Association Grid

might suggest in terms of a business. Start with automobile and run across the top making combinations for inspiration. For example:

Automobile   Perhaps a bookstore specializing in anything to do with automobiles— buying/selling/repairing; become a center and advocate for consumers who hate to buy automobiles; give referrals to fair dealers for a small commission; maybe a superstore that sells everything including parts, repairs, car insurance, alarm systems, car wash, clearinghouse for jobs in auto industry.

Books   Mail order book supplier to dentists and physicians, including technical books and financial and recreational books tailored for them; become an international center for books and information on fires of all kinds similar to The Center For Disease Control in Atlanta.

Carpet   Have a carpet-cleaning business oriented to janitors in apartment complexes; make them local agents for referrals.

Dentists   Organize a full-service business catering to dentists and physicians, and be a one-stop service center for decorating, repairs, insurance, cleaning, taxes, financial advisers; have all these associates lined up (not on salary) to respond.

Employment   Create a new policy for employment insurance that covers rent/mortgage when unemployed.

Do you catch the gist? Remember the Yellow Pages can be an incredible source of inspiration for business people. Fall in love with the Yellow Pages. You need not approach your problem as systematically as the association grid above. Do it randomly, regardless of your problem.

For example, go back to the challenge of selling one million tires and look at some of these ideas in the same categories.

Automobile	Connect with all the service stations in the area and give attendants $10 for any referral they make when pumping gas. Because they have to wait while the gas is going in, they might as well inspect the customers' tires and give them a referral when tires are needed. Multiply this by, say 500 gas stations, and it could be fruitful.
Janitors	Make janitors in apartment complexes bird dogs. As they inspect the grounds of their facility, they can also inspect tenants' tires and refer those in need to you.
	In fact, this raises an interesting question as to who else could be bird dogs and refer business to you. Perhaps, parking attendants; the homeless who are wandering the streets anyway; the unemployed; grade school and high school kids; mail carriers; anyone working in a shopping center (at lunch break); inspection station employees who could tell you who flunked inspection because of bad tires.
Carpet	Flatten competition with unbeatable prices and service; weave add-ons into

the sale, e.g., extended warranties, free rotation of tires; cover a section of town wall to wall and use a multiprong, multimedia, blitzkrieg to generate interest, and then move to the next section.

And so on…. What is implied in this process is that anything can be a fishhook. Anything can stimulate another idea. So when you are looking for inspiration, creative stimulation, a fishhook—play with the Yellow Pages. Cast the line out and see what you can catch.

OTHER APPLICATIONS

The same principle works for any other kind of list, or glossaries in the back of books, or directories, or *Thomas' Register*, for example, or magazines, and the like.

The way this can work best for you is to clarify your problem by starting at the end, as suggested earlier, and posing it in a question. For example:

How can we sell one million tires?
What needs exist out here that people would be willing to pay to have addressed?
How can we motivate our salespeople to open new accounts and not just call on comfortable old accounts?
How can we find the right person for this job?

INCUBATION

Once you have formulated the problem in a question, stop consciously thinking about the problem, and go about your other business, or play sports, run, relax— do something else!

Is your brain still working on the problem? Yes. Imagine that while you are off preoccupied with something else you delegated the job of searching for an answer to someone else, and that someone else works right around the clock searching for the solution to your problem.

Now that is efficient isn't it? You are off having fun, and the research is still being done. Well, that is exactly the way the brain works, and it is easier to understand by continuing our analogy to fishing.

1. You have a fisherman in your head—your subconscious mind.

2. To move the inner fisherman into fishing he needs an order.

3. When you consciously formulate your problem in a question form, it triggers the inner fisherman into action.

4. What does the inner fisherman do? He throws hooks into the lake and strives to pull out a big fish—a great idea.

5. Where do the hooks for the inner fisherman come from? Everywhere: outside—what you read, what you see, what you hear; inside—what you have experienced, seen, learned or felt. All of this is available to the inner fisherman as a hook.

6. Understanding this, you now know how to program him. You can do it any time during the day, evening or when it is especially productive, just before you slip off to sleep. Simply, put the problem you are working on in the form of a question, and drift off to sleep. While you sleep, your inner fisherman is fishing.

7. How do you know when your inner fisherman has caught a great idea? Because the inner fisherman can hardly contain himself when this happens, he pushes the ideas from the subconscious mind into conscious awareness. This can occur anytime, but is often accompanied by an exclamation like "aha!" "I've

got it!" "Eureka!" This is what is called the "Aha Experience." It is the solution to the problem or part of the problem and is experienced as a tremendous insight. When it occurs, it needs to be written down, played with, elaborated upon, and of course, brought into action.

ARE INSIGHTS ALWAYS CRYSTAL CLEAR?

Occasionally, you might wake up in the night with a tremendous insight. Immediately copy the insight down in detail. Then put it aside and deal with it in the morning.

When you look at it in the morning, it may look like gibberish or something that is not directly understandable. How do you deal with this? Regard it as an especially valuable fishhook that your inner fisherman has sent to the surface. Do not dismiss it from your conscious mind because it does not appear to make sense. Rather, use it as a fishhook to pull out of the lake other fish—other associations, other ideas.

Go back to the principle of association. Anything can be a fishhook to pull out an idea but because this fishhook came from your inner fisherman in response to your question, it is especially valuable. So play with it; see what else it stimulates. Put it away for awhile, then come back to it. You will find something of significant value when you do.

SUMMARY

To summarize the incubation process, remember creativity occurs at two levels: the conscious and the subconscious.

The following is a simple process flow chart that identifies what is going on at the conscious and the subconscious levels.

These charts will show you what the conscious fisherman does to become more creative and what the subconscious fisherman is doing. You will note immediately that the conscious fisherman formulates the problem as a question and then diverts the individual's attention to a point where one eventually captures insights. The problem as a question becomes the chief prodder, the element that sets it all in motion.

At the same time, the subconscious is hard at work too. The subconscious raises a question that triggers fishing and that eventually leads to hooking a good fish. When it's ready to be reeled in, it sends that up to the conscious.

The bottom line here is that you must be a two-handed fisherman. You must do both: you are working on two levels both consciously and subconsciously.

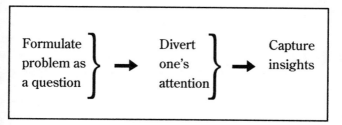

Figure 7:
What Does the Conscious Fisherman Do To Become More Creative?

1. The problem as a question is the great actuator.

2. Divert conscious attention to play or something relaxing.

3. When insights bubble up, write them down.

While this is going on, what is the subconscious fisherman doing? See *Figure 8.*

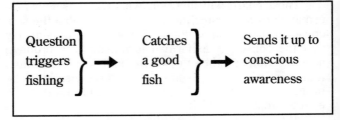

Figure 8:
What The Subconscious Is Doing

So be a fisherman both consciously and subconsciously.

CHAPTER 8

ANALOGIES AS FISHHOOKS

Comparison Leads to Discovery

> ## *"Metaphor is probably the most fertile power possessed by man."*
>
> —Jose Ortega Y Gasset

You will note in the preceding chapter I developed the analogy of fishhooks. I think using the analogy between your memory, creativity and idea generation to a lake, fish, and fishing is a fruitful way to help you understand the need to exercise initiative in problem solving. To catch fish you need fishhooks; to get ideas you need to know how to provoke ideas.

Analogies can be among the most fertile fishhooks we can use. By taking the subject and comparing it to something else, that something else becomes a multiple fishhook. All we need to do, for example, is to amplify what the fishhook is and does and each one of these attributes will suggest something new about the subject of comparison. For example, when comparing fishing to creativity in *Figure 9*, observe the array of attributes associated with fishes, fishing, and fishhooks in the left column. Then look at the ideas that they suggest about creativity in the right column.

Why use an analogy to stimulate creativity? Often they help us to explain, understand, guide and direct our thinking in ways we would not have thought of otherwise. For example, if we say, "Life is just a bowl of cherries," what are the associations we immediately

Attributes of Fishes, Fishing, & Fishhooks	Ideas About Creativity
Lake teeming with fish	abundance of possibilities
Looking for something to eat	ideas need to be provoked
Some fishhooks have bait	some ways to stimulate ideas more fruitful than others
Others don't have bait	throw up random stimuli
Need a fisherman	need someone interested in the process
Need a variety of fishhooks	variety of provocations
Some fish you throw back in	not all ideas are good ones

Figure 9:
Comparing Fish To Creativity

make? Life is fun, good, energizing, a dessert, and juicy. Notice the difference between the statement, "Life can be a very positive experience" and "Life is just a bowl of cherries." The first is a classic left brain abstract unidimensional statement. The other is what poetry is made of—it consists of a multi-dimensional fishhook that can provoke a range of responses in the user.

How can we use an analogy to help solve a problem? Suppose, for example, you, as the CEO of your company, want to build a great company and you want to motivate your employees to outstanding performance. Remember the model:

1. Start at the end: The end is to become a great company.
2. State your problem in the form of a question: "How can we become a great company?"

Now, notice the different kinds of ideas that come to mind depending on which analogy, you, as the CEO, use.

We are a team.
We are a family.
We are in a battle.
We are growing a business.
We are building a great company.
We are pioneers.
We are high rollers.
We live to serve.
We are all salespeople.
We are in a competitive jungle.
It is a dog eat dog world.
Winning is everything.
The market is in the doldrums.

Which analogy the CEO uses can spawn a lot of ideas that can help his employees make it happen. For example, suppose he said: "To be a great company we need to be a great team."

Once the array of attributes are out there, the CEO could choose the strong ones. The CEO can then spawn parallel persuasion points that relate to the task of becoming a great company, their role, their behavior, their relationships, and their attitudes.

By using the team analogy, however, you can see how it guides, directs, and suggests points to emphasize in a motivational talk.

If the CEO chose another analogy, e.g., warfare, jungle, family, pioneers, or the like, a whole other set of attributes and another set of persuasion points would have been emphasized.

HOW ELSE WE COULD USE ANALOGY

Suppose we want to improve sales by 30% by year's end. (Start at the end) Put it into a question:
"How can we improve sales 30% by year's end?"

It is a game.
We want to win.
The rewards go to the winner.
Losers get sent to the minors.
A team is: unified
             integrated
             single-minded
             more than the sum of its parts
             energetic
             positive
             expects to win
Team members: cooperate with each other
                respect each other
                support each other
                do their job without being asked
                are highly skilled at their special job
                identify with the team
                have positive feelings towards one an-
                    other
                enjoy what they are doing
                encourage one another
It is tense
It is a struggle
Competition: is also a team and highly skilled
               wants to win
               is highly motivated

Figure 10:
Attributes Associated with a Team

Let us compare improving sales to something specific, i.e., improving sales is like:

Climbing a mountain
Selling umbrellas when it is raining
Carving a marble statue
Throwing a dinner party
The Normandy invasion
A beauty contest
A game of pool
The voyage of Kon-Tiki

Remember what we are looking for: ways to improve sales. Let us use: Improving sales is like carving a marble statue.

The artist needs a clear vision
Needs tools such as chisels, brushes
Needs perseverance
Needs good materials
Needs help from others
Needs skill at carving
Needs help to get block in position
Needs to clean up periodically

Figure 11:
Attributes of Carving a Marble Statue

What ideas do they suggest to improve sales? Here are some possibilities:

Perhaps the salespeople could learn the skill of visualization in order to deepen their motivation and sense of purpose.

Perhaps they could get better capability brochures; or laptop computers with color screens.

Perhaps they could go back and call on everybody they called on in the first half of the year.

Perhaps we could take some factory people to customers to show them the problems of quality on-site.

Perhaps we could send everyone to an advanced sales training course.

Perhaps we could lessen paperwork and move to direct-order entry.

Perhaps we could visit dissatisfied customers in person.

We could go on and on, but the method is simple—the attributes of the thing compared suggest ideas to solve the problem.

IMPLAUSIBLE ANALOGIES

In the preceding examples the comparisons between the two subjects have been plausible, for example, between fishing and creativity; between carving a marble statue and improving sales. There is another way to stimulate creativity that is easier, albeit apparently illogical, and that is to compare your subject to something implausible. For example: improving sales is like melting ice; being caught in a dust storm; walking a tightrope backwards.

How do you use implausibility? Once you understand the principle of creativity—anything can be a fishhook—then anything can stimulate an idea. Therefore, ask yourself: "What are the attributes of melting ice?" Then, list them:

It is cold
Need to warm it up
Need a higher temperature
Transforms from one state to another
It is tangible and concrete
It is in flux

Figure 12:
Attributes of Melting Ice

Then ask: "How can this help me improve sales?" Perhaps the following:

Customers need to be warmed up.

I need to find ways to allow them to get comfortable with me.

Customers are in flux; have lots of obligations; have their problems to solve. Maybe I could help them to solve some, or many, of their problems.

If I don't find ways to warm them up, the chances of making a fruitful connection are remote.

Finding ways to warm up the customer has to
be the highest priority.

Perhaps I can warm them up by making them
indebted to me, e.g., a gift, a favor, lunch.

Research the company's problems—give away
solutions.

These are just a few possibilities—but remember
the principle: Fishhook, attributes of the fishhook, and
what do they suggest to solve your problem?

SUMMARY

The fruitfulness of using analogy to suggest ideas has
been explained. Why they can be used to stimulate creativity is summed up in another analogy, i.e., they are
fruitful. Test it out, and see what your experience is.

CHAPTER 9

AMPLIFY EVERYTHING WITH QUANTUM LEAP THINKING

Breaking Out of the Familiar Forces Creativity

"Imagination is more important than knowledge."

—Albert Einstein

S o far you have been exposed to three techniques that by themselves can provoke a myriad of ideas to resolve a problem. Another way to amplify creativity is to reconfigure the problem so that it is impossible to approach the solution-finding in the manner you typically would follow.

The manner we have in mind is *Quantum Leap Thinking*. It is one of the most fertile methods of generating ideas, and is a context in which creation can flow freely from an entirely different perspective.

AN EXERCISE OF IMAGINATION

To understand Quantum Leap Thinking do an exercise with me using your imagination. Follow my instructions slowly, thinking as vividly as you can and, at the end, answer the questions that I ask. First, as you proceed through this mind trip, turn on all your senses—in your mind's eye see colors, hear the sounds, feel the textures, and your body, and smell the aromas that drift into your scene:

Imagine that you are walking up a black mac-adam path to a large red brick building. On the wall, in big bold letters, is the word: Gymna-sium. When you arrive at the double door en-trance, you pull open the right side door and enter. Across the hall, through another double door, is a huge open area with five basketball courts and a track around the perimeter. The floor is a light, shiny hard-wood maple and, as you walk across the floor, you can hear your own leather heels echoing. At the far end, you see six boys playing basketball and hear their muffled sounds.

Your nostrils catch the unmistakable smell of great effort. When you reach the other side of the gym, you walk to the room you are looking for. Over the door is a sign: Weight Lifting Room. You turn the silver knob and enter; the door shuts gently behind you. You look around the room and observe the variety of muscle-building ma-chines. At the far end of the room there is a table and on the table is a barbell. Next to the barbell is a sign that says: 200 pounds. You walk up to the table.

Now, I am giving you a challenge. When I give you the signal, lift the 200 pounds with all the power you can muster right over your head. All right, get set; plant your feet firmly on the floor; pick up the resin bag on your left—it ab-sorbs the moisture on your hands—grasp it as if you are making a snow ball; drop it back on to the table. Put both hands on your cross-piece. Get set. I will count down from three, and then say "lift!" At the word "lift" thrust that 200 pounds over your head.

OK, ready: three, two, one...hold it! I made a mistake; that is not a 200 pound weight—it is only 20 pounds. But please, let us lift it anyway when I give you the signal. OK, ready: three, two, one, lift! Hold it over your head; now bring it slowly down, and put it back on the table. Now step back, and if you would, answer these questions:

1. When I asked you to lift 200 pounds over your head, what did you think? How did you feel?
2. As you got yourself ready to lift 200 pounds, what were you thinking?
3. When I told you, Oops, it is only 20 pounds, not 200 pounds—but let us lift it anyway, what did you think? How did you feel? What did you do?

Now, what does all this have to do with Quantum Leap Thinking and with creativity? Everything. Suppose, for example, your baseline goal was to lift 20 pounds, and you psyched yourself up to lift ten times that or 200 pounds. By stretching your mind and imagination to a grander challenge, the baseline challenge was hardly a challenge. Now, to lift 20 pounds is not a great challenge for most people to start with. But suppose the baseline challenge was, indeed, a stretch. By shooting way beyond the baseline goal, it makes it appear easier.

THE SALES EXPERIENCE

Most companies have observed that after a number of years salespeople tend to hit a plateau. That becomes their comfort zone. Partly this is a consequence of one of the perverse "rewards" salespeople receive for high performance: namely their quota for the following year gets ratcheted up. After a while salespeople (and this may not even be conscious), in effect, say "enough!" Thus, they plateau.

Part of their problem is simply this: Suppose this year their target is $1,000,000 in sales volume, and they hit it; in the second year, it becomes $1,100,000; in the third, $1,210,000, and by the time the seventh year is completed, the quota for the following year is almost double, $2,000,000 in sales volume. If they are still using the same methodology to go after $2,000,000 as they did to achieve $1,000,000 in sales, they wind up working longer hours, with more pressure, more stress, more phone calls, more paper work, more rejections, and more pain. So to put their life back in balance, they balance their achievement in sales with their pain, and hit a happy stride which we call "the comfort zone."

Now, how can salespeople turn themselves on and continue to grow? They can do Quantum Leap Thinking! How?

1. Clarify the baseline goal, e.g., sales quota.
2. Convert it into a Quantum Leap goal by putting it on a grander scale. Since the baseline goal, in the example above, was readily quantifiable, multiply it by 10, e.g., $1,000,000 × 10 = $10,000,000. Ten Million is the Quantum Leap Goal.
3. Make believe the Quantum Leap Goal is really the goal you have to hit, and your style of life, your family's well being, and your survival depend on your achieving it. This requires a giant leap of imagination. Do it by suspending your disbelief, and withholding any critical judgment—do it!
4. Spend a day generating ideas on how to accomplish the $10,000,000 target.

THE PAYOFF

A couple of interesting things happen as a consequence of this:

1. By trying to figure out how to hit a Quantum Leap Goal, a person might just succeed. You will never make a Quantum Leap if you never think about it.
2. Even if the achievement of a quantum leap goal is remote, invariably a person who puts a mind and

imagination to the task, will come up with an array of high-yield ideas.
3. When these ideas are plugged into the salesperson's baseline plan of action, it makes the achievement of the baseline goal a sure thing.
4. What is even more rewarding for the salesperson is that the baseline goal is no longer seen as an awesome challenge, but rather as a piece of cake.

SUMMARY

In summary then, what is the Quantum Leap Thinking Method?
1. Establish a baseline goal—a well-stated baseline goal follows this format: "To do how much of what by when."
2. Multiply it by ten; or if it is not readily quantifiable, put it on a grander scale—comparable to a ten times leap.

Below are examples of a variety of baseline goals escalated to a grander scale. Where they were readily quantifiable, it was done. Where they were not, analogous ways to put it on a grand scale were done.

Baseline Goal	Quantum Leap Goal
To visit the far west (USA) by end of 1992.	To visit far west, Hawaii, & Australia by the end of 1992.
To sell 2,000 chairs by 12/31/92.	To sell 20,000 chairs by 12/31/92.
To complete book by 10/31/93.	To complete 10 books by 12/31/93.
To reduce the cost of our product 10% by 12/31/93.	To reduce the cost of our product by 100% by 12/31/93.

Figure 13:
From Baseline Goal To Quantum Leap Goal

3. Make believe you have to achieve your Quantum Leap goal to survive. This requires a suspension of disbelief.

4. Looking at the Quantum Leap goal, ask yourself this question: In the entire scheme of the universe, is achieving this Quantum Leap goal *possible*? After due thought, you will discover that the answer to this question is: "YES!"

5. Spend a day (half-day, or at least a good piece of time) generating a long list of things you might do to achieve it. Use mind maps, the *Option Generator,* fishhooking, and analogies to prompt your creativity.

6. After you get a long list of ideas, choose the ones with particular merit and plug them into your plan of action designed to achieve your baseline goal.

ADVANTAGES OF QUANTUM LEAP THINKING

Quantum Leap Thinking forces a person to solve a problem in entirely new and different ways. Why? Because the usual or traditional ways of accomplishing the baseline goal would never prove adequate to the task of making a Quantum Leap goal. So, if the problem is that of accomplishing the Quantum Leap goal, it is necessary to think of something new. Working harder is not the answer; working smarter is a necessity.

Because most folks seem to be reluctant to stretch their imagination when it comes to improvement, Quantum Leap Thinking creates the necessity to do so. It can be, therefore, a powerful tool to encourage employees toward innovation.

APPLICATIONS

Sales: Because sales is the engine that drives the train, a good time to do Quantum Leap Thinking is in the fourth quarter of the year, when quotas for the following year are set. When sales people are exposed to this type of thinking, it reduces bad feelings, and pushes them enthusiastically into the next year with a raft of high-yield ideas they can't wait to implement.

Management: Most companies have some sort of Management By Objectives (MBO) program that also gets established in the fourth quarter. This is also a good time for them to take each separate objective, do a 10× factor, and spend time generating new possibilities.

As a consequence, the new plan for the following year will seem possible, and there is an outside chance they might even make a Quantum Leap. At any rate, high-yield strategies for achieving baseline results become evident.

Personal/Family Life: Apply the methodology to your health, finances, recreational life in a full-blown or in a modified manner, and you can get the same inspiring results.

ASSIGNMENT

The next time you are troubled over the solution to a problem, test out Quantum Leap Thinking.

CHAPTER 10

FROM IDEA TO ACTION

The Bridge from Creativity to Results

"Do It Now!
Do It When You Don't Feel Like It!
Do It Especially When You Don't Feel
Like It!"

—D.J. Noone

The techniques discussed such as questioning, mind maps, fishhooks, analogies, and Quantum Leap Thinking can help you generate many ideas. They can, in fact, give you a surfeit of riches and, with that, create a new problem: which idea makes the most sense?

There is an easy and somewhat effective way to decide this as well as more complex but thorough ways to do it. Both types will be explained and, depending on how much time you have available, you can choose which type makes the most sense for you.

THE EASY WAY

When you have an array of possible solutions, say, for example, ten—simply rank the solutions from 1 to 10, where 1 is the idea with the most merit and the others are put in order of decreasing merit. This simple process allows the strongest ideas to emerge.

In the process of selecting the highest-valued idea or ideas, feel free to modify them in any way that makes more sense. New insights can be incorporated anywhere along the path to finding a solution.

A MORE COMPLEX METHOD—THE BEN FRANKLIN METHOD

In order to analyze the relative merits of an idea, Ben Franklin would get a blank sheet of paper and put a line down the middle. On the left he would put a plus, while on the right he would put a minus. On the plus side, he would list all the advantages of the idea and on the negative side he would list all the disadvantages of the idea. Once all these judgments were in front of him, he could make an overall judgment as to the fruitfulness of the idea.

To use this approach in comparing one idea to other ideas, it is useful to make a quantitative judgment on the overall merit of the idea. Once again, use a scale from 1 to 10, where 10 is terrific. The whole plus-minus analysis can be summarized in a number, e.g., 9. When the plus-minus analysis of each idea is done and then summarized in a quantitative judgment, it thus becomes easier to determine which idea(s) has the most merit.

The advantage of this method is that all kinds of diverse criteria can be considered and still the analysis can be summarized in a quantitative judgment.

A MORE COMPLEX MULTI-VARIABLE METHOD

This method, although appearing complex, is a method that can deal with many, many ideas in a simple, systematic manner.

Criteria

First of all we need to determine what criteria to use in order to assess the value of an idea. There are six criteria I have found to be relevant (you may have special criteria that more readily fit your circumstance, use them):

Time: Since time is money, time refers to whether the implementation of the idea will take a long time or a short time. The quicker an idea can be implemented the better.

Risk: Every new direction has a chance of failing. When thinking of the risk factor, think about the cost of failure if it goes wrong. The smaller the cost of failure the better.

Effectiveness: Does the idea do the job? Is it the hammer to strike the nail? The more readily the idea allows you to achieve intended results the better is its effectiveness.

Investment: What kind of financial obligation does the idea require, and what is the potential return on the investment? The smaller the investment where the return is high, the better.

Ease of Implementation: Some things are simple and easy to do; other things require many steps, cooperation of many others, and tools/services that are sophisticated and complex. The easier an idea is to implement, the better.

Feeling Factor: This is the toughest criteria to quantify because it refers to intuition, a strong feeling that an idea is right, often in absence of proof. The more convinced you are intuitively that something makes sense, and when there is nothing to substantially disprove it, the more likely it is that your inner voice is saying: "Go for it!" When that happens, take it as a favorable sign.

With these criteria in mind, you could construct a simple evaluation format, like the one following:

Idea(s) To Be Evaluated	Time	Risk	Effect	Invest	Ease	Feel	TOTAL

Criteria

Figure 14:
Evaluation Criteria

The scales you use on the criteria can be based on simple judgments of plus or minus that you then add up to generate a total value of pluses and minuses. Ideally you are looking for an idea that scores six pluses.

When an array of ideas is compared, this quantitative summary makes it easier to determine the idea(s) that truly have merit. For example:

PROBLEM: How to improve sales?

Ideas To Be Evaluated   *Criteria*

	Time	Risk	Effect	Invest	Ease	Feel	TOTAL
							+ −
Take a customer to lunch	−	+	+	−	−	0	2 3
Give a gift	+	+	+	+	+	+	6

Figure 15:
Evaluating Sales Improvement Ideas

The weight of the analysis goes to "giving a gift."

A MORE PRECISE JUDGMENT

Once again, using a scale from 1–10, where 10 is terrific, you could make a quantitative judgment on each criteria, and then sum up the values to come up with an overall score. For example:

	Time	Risk	Effect	Invest	Ease	Feel	TOTAL
PROBLEM: How to improve sales?							
Ideas To Be Evaluated				*Criteria*			
Take a customer to lunch	3	9	8	3	4	3	30
Give a gift	9	9	6	3	3	3	33

Figure 16:
Evaluating Sales Improvement Ideas On 1–10 Scale

The weight of this analysis also goes to giving a gift. If there were other ideas, the totals would allow us to rank the ideas based on the analysis. The precision of the rank order is enhanced over the Easy Way of rank ordering because it is not based just on intuition but rather on a careful consideration of the same criteria for each idea.

HOW DO YOU MOVE AN IDEA INTO ACTION?

Once you have generated possible solutions and selected the one(s) that make sense, the next step is to make the idea actionable. This means to formulate the idea in a way that has "teeth"—in a way you can do something about! How do you take an idea like "take a customer to lunch" and give it teeth? An actionable idea with teeth follows this formula:

"Do how much of what by when at what cost."

In the case of "take a customer to lunch" this might be put this way:

Take eight customers to lunch each month, investing no more than $50 for each event.

Or in the case of "give a gift":

Give 25 key customers a book by October 1, costing no more than $20 each.

IMPORTANCE OF AN ACTIONABLE IDEA

The beauty of an actionable solution with teeth is that it is measurable, has a time frame (deadline) and a specific cost attached to it. It is, furthermore, concrete, specific, and you can tell if, indeed, the idea has been implemented. This contrasts to an unactionable idea that is vague, amorphous, abstract, and has no time frame or cost attached to it. So, if you want to make things happen, make your ideas actionable.

FROM ACTIONABLE TO ACTION

Once you have an actionable idea, it is useful to ask, "what steps do I need to take to implement it?" The answer to this question will spawn an array of action steps and will become the basis for your plan of action. For example, on the actionable idea, "take eight customers to lunch each month investing no more than $50 each event," what steps do I need to take? The answers are again formulated with teeth, in this instance "to do how much of what by when." Thus, some action steps might be:

1. Identify restaurants with class by 8/1.
2. Identify which customers to invite by 8/1.
3. Make a luncheon schedule by 8/3.
4. Call for eight appointments for September by 8/5.
5. Day before luncheon date call to confirm.
6. After the luncheon write down what I learned.
7. Develop, where appropriate, a plan for follow-up.

The rule of thumb when executing action steps that you find do not work is to simply ask: "What can I learn from this experience?" Then, *do something else*. Continue doing this "action, feedback, correction, action" method until the idea is implemented.

CONCLUSION

You now have the method for becoming a creative problem solver. You know how to define your problem, use questions, mind maps, association, analogies, and fishhooks, all within the frame of Quantum Leap Thinking. Once you get a great idea and implement it through careful steps—and sometimes through trial and error and retrial—you have the secret to achievement.

CHAPTER 11

WHEN PROBLEMS OVERWHELM

Strategies for Overcoming Distress

"To look up and not down,
To look forward and not back,
To look out and not in, and
To lend a hand."

—Edward Everett Hale

Occasionally, despite our best efforts, we arrive at a state of overload. It seems that we are being overwhelmed, or, to use a frightening analogy, we are being sucked deeper and deeper into quicksand that is up to our chin. A number of options are available, some of which are more useful than others:

1. *We can scream.* Although screaming has a certain cathartic effect by relieving some of the emotional pressure and might, indeed, make the reasonable part of our brain more available, it does not solve the problem of "overwhelm."

A related but less dramatic experience is to cry. "It is OK to cry"—and men especially need to give themselves this permission because it is, indeed, a healthy way to release the pressure, the feelings of being overwhelmed. Crying not only cleanses but, afterwards, it makes the reasonable part of the brain more available. So, if you haven't had a good cry lately, have one; it will improve your problem-solving capability.

2. *We can escape.* For example, we could lock the office door and physically remove ourselves from the environment associated with our major pressures. Sometimes this gives us relief and enables us to put things in bet-

ter perspective. As a forward step it is not without merit.

3. *We could anesthetize ourselves.* For example, through drink or drugs we can kill the pain of the "overwhelm." As common as the "happy hour" is, it is not recommended. There are, of course, other anesthetics people use to relieve tension, e.g., food, activity frenzies, smoking, nail biting—all negatives in excess.

There are, on the other hand, positive anesthesia or positive addictions, such as running, workouts, work, and sex, for example. When done in moderation these can be life enhancing. However, even these, when done excessively, can worsen a situation.

Nevertheless, the problem with anesthesia is that the relief from the pain of "overwhelm" is only temporary, and soon after the relief comes the pain again.

4. *We could do nothing.* For example, stare into space and allow ourselves to be "numbed out." This is like being in neutral but clouded with a dark, emotional gloom. No good things happen in this state because the physiological messages sent to the person's brain only serve to further de-energize and to deepen the pit of despair. Further, the person's demeanor saps the energy of everyone else around, and soon the contagion of discouragement pervades a family, group, or an organization.

The opposite of doing nothing is to do *something!* In the aftermath of Hurricane Andrew, which hit south Florida, a young man recounted his experience, describing how all the trees were down, there was no electricity or telephones, his roof was blown off, car destroyed, and all the roads were blocked with fallen trees. He and his wife were safe but, not having a chain saw, he found himself sawing branches from the trees with his little 10-inch hand-saw. He knew it was not very efficient, but he said he felt better doing something. As inefficient as it was, it was an advance over being "numbed out" and it was clearly more purposeful than what certain cavalries were known to do when in doubt, i.e., gallop.

5. *We can use the "pain shrinker."* Although this strategy, described subsequently, does not solve your problem(s), it does put it into perspective. Put your problem into perspective by asking the right questions. Here are four good ones:

a. How does this problem compare to all the other problems you have worked through in your life?

b. Project yourself into the future to the last day of your life, and ask yourself from that vantage point how does this problem compare?

c. Expand your frame of reference and consider how your problem compares to the starving people of Somalia, Sudan, Kenya, or the victims of Serbian attacks, or to others who are suffering worse pain than you have right now.

d. Lastly, think of the unfolding of human civilization from earliest times and reflect on the wars, the massacres, the holocaust, the floods, the earthquakes, tidal waves, volcanic eruptions, and ask yourself how your problem compares to these events.

The advantage of seeing your problem in perspective is that it puts you in a better position to do something about it.

6. *Make a Gratitudes List.* Another amazing thing to do to put your lot in perspective is to get a blank sheet of paper and pencil and at the top write: "What am I grateful for?" Then list below it all the things for which you are grateful. This is powerful because it shifts a person's focus from the negative to the positive side, from the pain to the things to be happy about. It is not possible for a person to be depressed and miserable while constructing a gratitudes list. When done, put the list on your refrigerator and read it every day. It helps to put you into a "feel good" state, and that is the state where creativity flourishes best.

7. *We can stop making condemning judgments.* This is a very powerful way to orient yourself toward solving the

problem. Emotions such as fear, worry, guilt, frustration, disappointment, and loss all flow from prior condemning judgments like: "It's wrong!" "It is not right!" "It shouldn't be!" "It shouldn't have happened!"

How do you *not* make a condemning judgment? When reflecting on your problem, instead of the condemning judgment, simply say to yourself: "It happened." "It's over." "It's behind me". "It is history." No condemning judgments, no anguish; your focus has shifted to the present and to what "is." You are now in a better position, without all the emotional flooding, to solve your problem.

Related to this is the futility of asking "Why?"—a classic endless loop question to which there is no answer. In fact, "Whys?" are a cry of anguish, and imply the unspoken condemning judgment, "It's not fair!" Iterations of "Why?" cement a person in powerlessness and a further sense of victimization.

The better part of wisdom is to ask empowering questions such as, "What can I do about my problem?"

8. *We can talk to someone who will listen.* Talking about your problem is a classic method of getting the stuff swirling around inside your head outside. This strategy often prompts the troubled person to own the problem and the solution and, in the process, provides an opportunity to vent feelings. This is why, in most instances, when this occurs, a person will feel better after a one-on-one talk than before having it.

The problem with talking is finding someone who knows how to listen. Many good people, when confronted with the opportunity to listen to someone with problems that have significant emotional content, will try to talk them out of the feelings, saying such things as "Don't be afraid." What is even more common is to hear lectures, moralizing, blaming, and criticism. Most of the time it is hard to find anyone who wants to even hear your story.

The proper way to listen is to listen with acceptance of the troubled person's feelings while striving to understand what they are experiencing. This is done by asking open-ended questions and biting your tongue before expressing non-acceptance of the feelings.

You can be a good friend when you listen to someone else who is overwhelmed. And if it is hard to find a friend who will do that for you, go to a professional—that is what they are trained to do. It will be worth the investment.

9. *Lend a hand.* As the quotation at the beginning of the chapter suggests, a great way to reduce our own sense of victimization is to reach out and help someone else. Simple acts of caring stretch us and energize us to more readily solve our own problem.

10. *We can sort it out.* Sorting things out is the strategy most recommended because it allows us to de-emotionalize the situation, brings order out of the converging chaos, and above all, gives us maximum control. Where do we start the process? Start with a mind map. A mind map allows us to capture the chaos in a graphic manner. This act externalizes the problem, gives us perspective immediately and releases the emotional pain straightaway. As you remember, you do a mind map without trying to impose any order, rationale, or sequence beyond connecting ideas that are stimulated by previous ideas. The focus question in this instance would simply be: "What is overwhelming me?" Note how it starts: A blank sheet of paper and a focus question with a circle around it.

Figure 17:
A Focus Question For One In "Overwhelm"

The rest is listening to yourself, capturing the categories in Key Words, and connecting them with a string to the focus question or, as it develops, to whatever other category might be connected. A fictitious sample of a person in "overwhelm" might look like *Figure 18.*

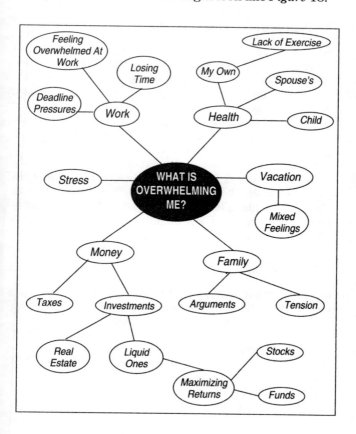

Figure 18:
Mind Map Of A Fictitious Person In "Overwhelm"

If you do a mind map, the next time you are in "overwhelm" or experiencing stress or upset of any kind, my guarantee is that you will feel better after you do it than you did before. Feeling better will then become the propelling force to achieve greater control.

WHAT COMES AFTER THE MIND MAP?

So, what next? The next step is simply to decide the order in which you want to deal with the problems. This decision does not imply that one category is more important than another category. For example, if you decide to deal with "money" first and "family" fourth, it does not mean "money" is more important than family matters. It simply means that in trying to get a better grip on things, you will deal with "money" first.

So let us suppose the order in dealing with the problems is: 1–money, 2–work, 3–health, and 4–family. In some respects, it does not matter in what order you choose to begin. The important point is to put the problems in any order. Then begin with number one, and end with the last category.

AN APPLICATION

In early September, 1992 Hurricane Andrew hit south Florida and wreaked horrendous devastation. I was asked by one of my clients to help the folks in the sales office in Coral Gables to cope better, as many of them had lost houses, had property destroyed, trees uprooted, were without electricity, and felt devastated by the hurricane. They also knew many other people who were even worse off.

Since I was not sure of the extent of the problems of the 14 people in detail, I organized a group session and had each do a mind map of their problems. When they completed the mind maps, I asked them to put their problems in the order that they had dealt with, or will deal with, them. Each person then explained the order which they decided upon. Afterwards, I taught them a few things from this chapter about solving problems, and each was afforded an opportunity for a one-on-one conversation with me to talk about the experience.

The upshot of this event is that in sharing the mind maps with the group a tremendous empathy was experienced by each person. Many felt they were no longer alone, and that their problems paled by comparison to others' problems. All of them were already on the upward slope to recovery when they showed up for the session and the exercises and opportunity for ventilation helped them to continue on an ascending path to further recovery. In conclusion, the strategies worked, and they can work for you.

AFTER PUTTING THE PROBLEMS IN ORDER

Now, back to the mind map and putting the problems in order. What next? Let us start with "money." By inspecting the mind map section on "money" an outline suggests itself.

```
Money
    Taxes
    Investments
        Real estate
                repairs
                selling
                rents
        Liquid ones
            maximizing returns
                stocks
                funds
```

Figure 19:
From Mind Map To Outline

Now with the outline in hand, it is useful to ask yourself about each category, "What do I want to make happen?"

For example:

Key Result Area	Intended Result
Money	Achieve a positive savings flow from all sources of $50,000 by the end of year.
Taxes	Complete plan to minimize taxes by 9/1.
Investments	Achieve a positive cash flow of $30,000 by end of year.
Real Estate	Complete R. E. plan by end of next week.
Repairs	List all repairs and contract by Fri.
Selling	Obtain three appraisals of property and choose one agent in two weeks.
Rents	Rent vacant apartment ASAP.
Liquid Investments	Maximize returns by selling losers in stocks and funds by tomorrow.

Figure 20:
What Do I Want To Make Happen?

You will note that each intended result is stated in a manner that has teeth, and follows the classic formula for any well-stated objective: "To do how much of what by when."

MORE PRECISION

If you need even more precision, you could then ask yourself about each intended result as specified: "What steps do I have to take to make it happen?" The answer to this question can be mind mapped, put in chronological order, and then stated in that order with teeth, i.e., "to do how much of what by when." This, then, is the basis for an action plan to achieve the intended result. You will note the similarity between this process and that of setting objectives and making plans in business.

You could then move to the next Key Result Area, i.e., #2–work, and proceed in the same manner, and then, likewise for #3–health, and #4–family.

It is important to note that to move out of the blue funk of "overwhelm," it is not necessary at the moment to develop fully any of the plans of action, no less all of them. From a minimalist perspective all that is necessary to feel better is to:

1. Mind map the causes of "overwhelm."
2. Decide the order in which you will deal with them.
3. Start dealing with whatever is number one.

WHY WILL YOU FEEL BETTER?

You will feel better because you are moving out from under the cloud of powerlessness. You will begin to feel that instead of sinking in a morass of deep quick sand, that you have found hard bottom and a way to start climbing out. You will feel there is hope. In effect, you are moving into a problem-solving mode.

Being in such a mode creates optimism, a better perspective and a sense of control. By externalizing the inner jumble of pressure through mind mapping the issues in the order in which you will deal with them, you control how you will think about them. These actions send an "overwhelmed" person the resounding message: "I can do something about this! In fact, I am doing something about my situation."

Powerlessness evaporates and, as the process continues to spell out specific goals and action steps, enthusiasm about moving into action develops. Action follows, solving the problem follows that, and success feeds on success. Pretty soon, being overwhelmed is only a memory and, if it occurs in the future, the method to vanquish it is known.

A CAVEAT

Years ago Sergeant Friday of *Dragnet*, a TV police drama, was known to say, "Just the facts, Ma'am." His much ridiculed line has merit in helping us to understand "overwhelm," because catastrophic thinking sends the mind galloping off into all the worst-case scenarios. Once a person becomes preoccupied not only with the internal chaos but also by the awful things assumed to be in store, the waves of pain do, indeed, become overwhelming. The fantasy thus becomes reality.

What is the antidote? Do as Sergeant Friday would do. Deal with the facts in front of you and refuse to be terrified by thoughts of impending and apparently inevitable doom. Remember, stick with the facts, realize that there is always a way, and finally, understand that there are no catastrophes. Adverse things that happen to you can be unfortunate, inconvenient, painful—but not catastrophic. This is true even of death, which if you define as the "next great adventure," ceases to panic such a definer. Once we adopt this view, like Little Orphan Annie, we clearly know there is always a "tomorrow."

CHAPTER 12

RULES FOR CREATIVE PROBLEM SOLVING

*Reminders and Homework
for the Rest of Your Life*

"Whoever becomes imbued with a noble idea kindles a flame from which other torches are lit, and influences those with whom he comes in contact, be they few or many."

—Henry George

REMINDERS

1. Accept stark reality—bad things happen.
2. Welcome problems as opportunities.
3. Suspend judgment as you generate possibilities.
4. Don't be a "but-head."
5. When generating ideas, go for quantity—quantity leads to quality.
6. Understand that different is not wrong, just different.
7. Avoid "go nowhere" questions; in particular, the "endless loop" ones.
8. Fine-tune your instrument by keeping your energy high.
   a. *Eat*—70/30: 70% fruits and vegetables; 30%, the rest.
   b. *Deep Breathe*—ten times, three times a day.
   c. *Move*—15 minutes of aerobic exercise a day, each day.
   d. *Relax*—20 minutes a day, two times a day.
   (*Even if you do not fulfill the ideal program, something is better than nothing*).
9. Put yourself into a resourceful state by firing off your anchor.

10. Ask empowering questions—often and many.
11. Post "The Option Generator" as a reminder.
12. Use mind mapping to get the dump out.
13. Use association, fishhooking, and analogy for inspiration.
14. Amplify achievement by using Quantum Leap Thinking.
15. Make sure your good ideas have teeth, and are actionable.
16. To achieve results, generate ideas, make a decision, plan, act, and observe feedback.
17. When something does not work, try something else; persist until you achieve intended results.
18. When problems overwhelm, adopt a multiple-strategy approach to feel better; keep Chapter 11 nearby.

A HOMEWORK ASSIGNMENT

1. Put these reminders in a high traffic area of your home/office.
2. Count the frequency with which you read these reminders in the course of a month.
3. Become a student of creativity and continue your search to find ways to liberate yourself even more.
4. To learn more about problem solving, go teach someone else some of the things you have learned here.

BY YOURSELF OR IN A GROUP

The techniques in this book are applicable either to just yourself, alone or to groups. The one thing a group needs, however, is a group leader who understands the importance of separating the creative generation of ideas from evaluation. If evaluation of an idea occurs as it is thrown on the table, creativity dies. It is like trying to drive with one foot on the accelerator and one on the brakes. Therefore, a group leader has to be adamant about keeping idea generation separate from idea evaluation and fine anyone during the idea generation $1 each time that person is a critic or a "But-head." Also, the leader should make sure everyone in the group is regularly asked to contribute.

FAREWELL

Good luck. Have many problems, welcome them, and create a better place for you and yours, and others.

SUGGESTED READING

Adams, James. *Conceptual Blockbusting*. Norton: New York, 1980.

Bailey, Covert. *The New Fit Or Fat*. Houghton Mifflin: Boston, 1991.

Benson, Herbert. *The Relaxation Response*. Morrow: New York, 1975.

Buzan, Tony. *Use Both Sides Of Your Brain*. Dutton: New York, 1974.

De Bono, Edward. *Serious Creativity*. Harper Business: New York, 1992.

Gallwey, Timothy and Kriegel, Bob. *Inner Skiing*. Bantam: New York, 1979.

Hendler, Sheldon. *The Oxygen Breakthrough*. Morrow: New York, 1989.

Kriegel, Robert and Patler, Louis. *If It Ain't Broke... Break It!* Warner: New York, 1991.

LeBoeuf, Michael. *Imagineering*. McGraw-Hill: New York, 1980.

Osborn, Alex. *Applied Imagination*. Scribner: New York, 1979.

Ostrander, Sheila, and Schroeder, Lynn. *Superlearning*. Laurel: New York, 1979.

Prince, George. *The Practice of Creativity*. Collier: New York, 1970.

Raudsepp, Eugene. *Growth Games For The Creative Manager*. Perigee: New York, 1987.

Ray, Michael, and Myers, Rochelle. *Creativity in Business*. Doubleday: Garden City, NY, 1986.

Thompson, Chic. *What A Great Idea!* Harper Perennial: New York, 1992.

Von Oech, Roger. *A Whack On The Side Of The Head*. Warner: New York, 1983.

INDEX

TITLES THAT GENERATE SUCCESS!

Business Success Series

Fifteen titles comprise Barron's innovative series designed to help the business person succeed! All offer advice and facts on how to master job techniques that will generate success. Each book: Paperback, $4.95, Canada $6.50, 96 pp., 4³⁄₁₆" × 7"